BODYWORK FOR HORSES

Susan McBane

BODYWORK FOR HORSES

TECHNIQUES YOU CAN USE YOURSELF

SP

DISCLAIMER

The content of this book is provided for interest and information. The publisher and author cannot be held responsible in any way for the results of applying the techniques or using the information contained herein. It cannot be emphasised too strongly that the book is in no way intended to substitute or replace professional help from a veterinary surgeon, farrier, teacher or therapist. Its purpose is to help readers to help their horses as part of an integrated management regime to promote their well-being and health. At all times, it is recommended that readers seek expert advice before implementing therapies or techniques. Be aware always of safety: horses are unpredictable animals and handling and riding or driving them is potentially dangerous. Readers should take appropriate safety precautions to safeguard themselves, their horses and other people and animals.

Copyright © 2005 Susan McBane

First published in the UK in 2005
by The Sportsman's Press, an imprint of Quiller Publishing Ltd

British Library Cataloguing-in-Publication Data
A catalogue record for this book
is available from the British Library

ISBN 0 904057 48 9

Printed in Singapore

The Sportsman's Press
an imprint of Quiller Publishing Ltd.
Wykey House, Wykey, Shrewsbury, SY4 1JA, England
Tel: 01939 261616 Fax: 01939 261606
E-mail: info@quillerbooks.com
Website: www.swanhillbooks.com

CONTENTS

DEDICATION

This book is dedicated to the memory of Wendy Carr,
a lovely and strong lady whom I liked and greatly admired and who died just as this
book was nearing completion.

Wendy and her skewbald gelding, Jacob

ACKNOWLEDGEMENTS

My sincere thanks go to everyone who has helped me with this book, not only Andrew Johnston of Quiller Publishing, John Beaton, my copy editor, and Pauline Finch and Joy Claxton for the line drawings, but also the following people and horses. Pauline and Rose; Sheila and Sabio; Barbara; Janet and Lucy; Kay and Maddie; Tracey and Cyril; Sylvia and, posthumously, Pedro, Adel, Hussein and Nero; Dawn and Rouche; Yvonne and Fred; Vick, Julia, Mel and Theo.

INTRODUCTION

It is a sad but true fact that most of the problems our horses and ponies experience occur because they are domesticated and worked by us. It is probably true that if they were not useful to man (not solely beautiful to look at and good to be with) they would become nothing but curiosities in zoo parks and reserves and exist in relatively small numbers. The fact that they *are* part of our wide society in so many ways places the onus on us to look after them, and there are many ways of doing that.

This book is an introduction to those physical, 'hands-on' therapies and management techniques which owners can learn and apply safely to their horses themselves, preferably with some initial training from a qualified therapist. There are no machines involved and no drugs, just a pair of hands, common sense and the development of 'feel'. When the management and rehabilitation techniques of leading in hand, lungeing and long-reining are discussed, it is assumed that owners will already have much of the equipment needed – so there is little or no financial outlay involved in order to learn and apply the principles given here.

It is most important to never try to force a horse to accept a technique or submit to a therapy as this is when situations dangerous to both horse and handler can develop. In any case, force is contrary to the basic ethos of many therapies: if the horse does not co-operate the therapy may not be so effective. With gradual progress and patience, trust is built up and the partnership may gain much more than simply the effects of the technique or therapy. This does not mean that horses may not be safely tied up or restrained, often just by being held by a quiet, firm and confident person, but force such as strapping up a leg, twitching or certainly sedating and other methods are best left to professionals when, for instance, essential veterinary treatment is needed.

The past twenty years or so has seen great strides taking place in the horse industry as regards therapies other than conventional or orthodox veterinary medicine. Horse owners have always needed their veterinary surgeon and farrier but now we are aware of a much wider range of specialists and therapists who can help us to not only treat our horses when they have problems but also help to keep them healthy and less prone to injury and illness in the first place.

Probably the first 'extra' specialists who became seen more and more in stable yards were the 'horse dentist' and the 'back man', neither of whom would be qualified because qualifications did not exist for them decades ago. Farriers often rasped horses' teeth and back men often appeared to work wonders for horses with obscure lameness and movement problems. (Although it is strictly against the law now in the UK and some other countries, unqualified back men still work on horses without a referral from a veterinary surgeon and some do seem to have a gift for helping their patients.)

Even as recently as fifty to seventy-five years ago, farriers regularly treated horses for ailments of all sorts even though the profession of veterinary surgeon was well established by then. Centuries ago farriers treated horses for their ailments because there were no vets. and I remember acquiring as a child an early Victorian book which I pored over for hours, called *Clater's Horse Doctor* sub-titled *Every Man His Own Farrie*r featuring practices (aimed at treatment and other less well-intentioned practices) ranging from the still-familiar to the absolutely horrific.

Now equine dental technicians have their own formal training courses and qualifications and back men, although still existing, are being superseded by physiotherapists, osteopaths, chiropractors and massage therapists not to mention other practitioners in modalities such as acupuncture, acupressure and shiatsu which are all closely related energy therapies.

Physiotherapy with its wide range of treatments was the first 'alternative' therapy to become accepted by the veterinary profession but few would now deny a horse and owner a referral to a qualified osteopath or chiropractor or, indeed, to a practitioner of any recognised therapy. Vets vary in their views of such therapies: some believe in them or at least accept that they can be beneficial but others feel that they are a waste of the owner's time and money. However, from my experience and observation, it is rare for a vet to refuse a referral.

Some years ago, I bought an elderly Thoroughbred mare whom I felt would benefit from various complementary therapies. My excellent orthodox vet told me that he thought I'd be lucky to get her through the approaching winter. We had an equine profile (blood check) done and various disorders were put right with conventional treatments. Later, I requested that I be allowed to call in an osteopath because the mare could not reach round far to the left, and to have her treated by a medical herbalist and a homoeopathic vet. All these things were agreeable to my vet who was particularly interested to watch the osteopath at work (he had to attend to sedate the mare for the manipulations).

The conventional and complementary treatments all worked together on different aspects of the mare's problems and I ended up owning, riding and adoring her for three more years. Her problems disappeared or were greatly lessened and she seemed much more comfortable and relaxed. The vet said: 'whatever you're doing, just keep doing it' so I did until old age ultimately got the better of her at the age of twenty-six. It comes to us all if we live long enough.

You don't have to compete hard with your horse to realise that things very easily go wrong with them. The famous statement by a little boy, when asked what he knew about horses, to the effect that 'one end bites, the other kicks and there's always something wrong with the bit in the middle' seems very true at times. Veterinary expenses seem to rise and rise mainly, we are told, because of the cost of drugs and dressings and of running a modern-day practice, and most owners these days are prudent enough to have vet's fees insurance even though it can be a minefield to negotiate.

I find that this is actually having a dangerous effect in that some people are putting off calling in the vet when they should because they are afraid that in the year following the ailment their premium will shoot up and they usually find that their horse is not covered for a problem the company has previously paid out on, or even for related problems. This surely is a short-sighted policy on the insurers' parts because many people are now feeling that insuring for veterinary fees is not worthwhile. In either case, the horses are often going without essential veterinary treatment because, for one reason or another – personal finances or lack of insurance – owners simply cannot pay for it.

Some insurance companies do include an element in their payments for complementary/alternative therapies such as physiotherapy (which is actually mainstream now), osteopathy, chiropractic, homoeopathy, acupuncture, herbalism and others but it is limited, and an owner who wants to make regular use, when applicable, of such therapists may well be prevented from doing so by the fees which have to be paid. Not many owners, for instance, can afford to pay an acupuncturist around £50 to £75 per treatment when several sessions may be needed.

Other therapists may charge similar amounts and in a complex case it may be advisable to use more than one different type of therapy. The veterinary surgeon is needed to diagnose the initial problem (in the UK, for instance, only veterinary surgeons are allowed by law to actually diagnose). If it is decided that the horse has injured back muscles and associated soft tissues such as connective tissue, tendons and ligaments, he might prescribe painkillers and advise physiotherapy as well. A remedial farrier might be needed to shoe the horse in a different way to help him if he has been moving in an unnatural way to compensate for his pain and, following recovery, a weekly or monthly expert massage may be recommended to help keep the horse supple and pain free.

All this is fine for a professional yard, a competition yard with sponsorship or owners for whom money is not a problem, but most owners do not operate at this level and simply cannot afford the regular services of such people however much they love their horse and want the best for him. The result is that the horse usually goes without the benefits of these specialists and their particular therapies completely.

This is not necessary. There is no reason why an intelligent, conscientious owner cannot acquire a practical, working knowledge of various therapies and management techniques and engage professional therapists on a less frequent basis. I actually exclude veterinary surgeons from this remark because I believe that you should never skimp on your vet's services.

It is important that you have a good working relationship with your vet (who should be your first port of call), and with the professional therapist in whatever modality your horse needs at a particular time. Because of the legal situation regarding veterinary diagnosis, some non-veterinary therapists are extremely cagey about what they will even tell you about your horse's problem let alone what they will show you in the form of exercises and moves to help him. A good therapist should be willing to explain the treatment given and show you some simple techniques you can use to carry on their work or apply to your horse on a health maintenance basis or to assist recovery or rehabilitation.

Bodywork can be described as physical techniques which you do to the horse's body, from grooming to massage, from aromatherapy to shiatsu. The Contents page gives details of what is covered in this book.

The therapies and management techniques have been specifically chosen for their relative ease (with a reasonable amount of personal application and common sense) with which owners can apply them to their own horses. If you carry them out carefully and under professional supervision to set you off, you should certainly benefit your horse and increase his well-being.

Apart from the practical benefits, working on your horse in this way strengthens the bond of affection and understanding between you, the techniques will make the horse feel good and you will feel proud that you have mastered some simple but effective therapy at a modest level and helped your horse, so you both benefit. The real benefit comes when you make this new or enhanced way of managing your horse a regular part of your routine.

I am a trained equine shiatsu practitioner and am happy to teach owners various things to do to help their horses. I find it disappointing, though, when they admit that they are not carrying them on because they are too busy or because they did not feel it was 'helping' the horse – usually because they gave up! Even one session of any therapy or technique will make the horse feel better and regular treatments soon show full benefit in really helping to 'cure' or prevent mental and physical illness and injury. You would not expect your horse to stay clean and glowing if you only groomed him once a week or to get fit if you did not carry out his fitness programme. It is just the same with therapies: if you don't apply them they won't work!

Where disorders do occur, professional help plus consistent application of a specific therapy or technique, where appropriate, will help the horse back to health and soundness as effectively and quickly as possible.

Thorough training in any therapy is time-consuming and expensive and it would be wrong to suggest that an owner can become sufficiently expert in a short time to be able to treat his or her horse as effectively as a professional, but the owner can certainly help on a practical, support level to promote good health and condition, to help horses do the best they can with the bodies they have, to help prevent injuries occurring and to enhance healing and rehabilitation when they do occur.

For nearly every therapy described in this book, full books have been written so readers can fairly easily read up in depth on any which particularly interest them. If you do have an interest in any particular modality, reading further about it and learning to apply it on an owner basis may encourage you to attend, say, a weekend seminar or course on it to improve your knowledge and effectiveness. This, in turn, may even result in your deciding to train to become a professional. It was my interest in acupuncture which led me to train, initially at an 'owner' level, in shiatsu which is a related therapy. I enjoyed it so much, and found it so effective, that I trained, with the late Pamela Hannay, to a level at which I could work professionally to help other people's horses.

There is so much that can be done to help horses which is overlooked by owners. I hope this book will whet its readers' appetites to look further into this rewarding field, whether they wish to work on and help only their own horses or become professional therapists.

What is covered

You will see that the book is divided into four sections: (1) basic anatomy and physiology or how the horse is constructed (as far as you need to know for these therapies and techniques) and how its body works, (2) simplified injury and healing processes, (3) management and care techniques and (4) actual therapies.

Particularly in the section on management and care techniques of bodywork, readers may be surprised to see something as everyday as grooming but, done caringly, it is a form of light massage and a stimulator of the body's life force or energy. There are also techniques like wisping which many of today's younger generation know nothing about, lungeing and long-reining which are usually thought of only as means of exercising and training, suitable riding as a healing process and bodily improvement technique and even leading in hand – yes, even that can be done in a way which will help to heal body and mind.

OPPOSITE: *Pauline Finch and her Fell Pony mare, Waverhead Rose, regularly practice various aspects of bodywork for horses. Rose has very much a mind of her own and Pauline is convinced that the bodywork and classical riding together have strengthened and deepened their bond. They still have their arguments but manage to compromise over most things*

I hope this book will give you a new and different view of your horse and everyday techniques which you may have previously taken for granted or not fully understood. I hope it will also give you the confidence to apply actual therapies to him which you may never have thought of or believed you could never master. As the giver of healing, relief and pleasure, you will be surprised at how much they benefit you, too.

SECTION 1

BASIC ANATOMY AND PHYSIOLOGY

The Skeleton

The horse's body is based on its bony skeleton. The skeleton is the framework around which are the various soft tissues – muscles, tendons, ligaments and fascia or connective tissue – which are together responsible for holding the skeleton together and for moving it.

The skeleton is responsible for the horse's conformation, his make and shape, and its format is largely determined by genetics but also nutrition. He will take after his sire and dam and their ancestors. Given adequate to good nutrition when he is in his dam's womb and when he is growing (which he may do until the age of six or even seven), and ample opportunity to exercise, his skeleton will develop to its optimum capacity and strength.

Sadly for many horses and ponies, poor nutrition (which means not only inadequate levels of necessary nutrients but also proportionately imbalanced nutrients) results in stunted or abnormal growth or growth and development which do not reach their full, genetic potential. Over feeding is as bad as under feeding in this respect.

Bones

The main minerals needed for good skeletal development and maintenance are calcium, phosphorus and some magnesium. Bone is made up of these which integrate with fibrous, protein tissue. As the horse is growing up and maturing, the long bones in the legs grow from their ends from softer structures called 'growth plates'. These cover the ends of bones and are made mainly of a cushioning, rubbery substance made of protein and carbohydrate called cartilage which gradually gives way to bone by the action of special cells in the plates.

Young horses' bones are about two-thirds protein, making their bones softer and more flexible than those of old horses whose bones are about two-thirds minerals and so much harder and more brittle. The strongest bones are those of horses in adulthood and early middle age, say roughly from about seven years of age to around twelve or thirteen years of age.

Bone is far from 'set' when the horse becomes mature. It changes according to the demands made on it, becoming weaker or stronger with lessening and increasing stresses respectively. This process is called 'remodelling'. Bone also contains channels through which blood and lymph vessels pass and also nerves, all of which are needed to maintain bone health and remodelling. The long bones contain in their virtually hollow centres the bone marrow where blood cells are made.

Bones come in various shapes and sizes. As well as the so-called long bones of the limbs, there are

- small, squarish bones in the knees and hocks which help to absorb concussion
- flat bones which are thin and found in the skull and the shoulder blades
- pneumatic bones in the head which contain sinuses or air spaces for lightness
- sesamoid bones which act as pulleys over which run tendons in protective sheaths of tissue; they are found not only in the fetlocks towards the back but also in the feet (the navicular bone), the stifle (the patella or kneecap) and behind the knee (the accessory carpal or pisiform bone)
- irregular bones, the vertebrae in the spine, which have 'a hole in the middle' so that, when set together in a column, as they are, there is a channel running all the way down the spine in which the spinal cord (nerve tissue) runs from the brain to part way down the tail. There are indentations between the vertebrae to allow for the passage of nerves branching off from the spinal column and passing out with further branches all over the body.

Joints

Without joints, of course, the body would not be able to move. There are three main types of joint in the body – moveable, slightly moveable and fixed.

Moveable joints:
These typically comprise two bone-ends covered by cushioning cartilage and lubricated by synovia or joint oil. This is produced by the inner lining of the joint sac, a capsule of tissue surrounding and 'sealing' the entire joint. There are:

- hinge joints, such as the elbow, which permit significant movement in one plane only
- ball-and-socket joints such as the hip; said to allow for movement in more than one plane, sideways movement of the hip is restricted in the horse and can be quite painful if forced, such as during shoeing or travelling when the horse braces his legs to balance
- gliding joints as in the stifle, hock and knee where bones glide over one another
- pivot joints such as those between the skull and the two top vertebrae (the atlas and the axis) which allow the horse to turn and toss his head

Slightly moveable joints
These are the joints between the vertebrae in the spine. Between the vertebrae are thick pads or 'discs' of cartilage to protect the articular (touching and moving) surfaces. These enable the spine to move a little both horizontally and laterally.

Fixed joints
These are very firm, fused joints which, in practice, almost form one bone of the two they join.

They are found in the skull (which contains 37 bones!) and the sacrum or croup which is made up of five fused vertebrae with no flexion possible.

Very often, when a horse twists a leg or over-stresses a leg, it is the tissues around the joint which are injured. Over-use also favours the development of osteoarthritis which occurs when cartilage is damaged or badly worn. Joint infections can also result in osteoarthritis as the infection attacks the cartilage.

Ligaments

Ligaments come in various shapes and lengths. They are cords, sheets or bands of fibrous tissue with hardly any elasticity in them. They usually connect bone to bone or cartilage to bone. They are poorly supplied with blood vessels but amply supplied with nerves, and ligament injuries are very painful.

Their job is to bind together the bones of the skeleton and provide support for the whole framework of the horse's body, aided sometimes by muscles and also by other tissue called fascia or connective tissue.

Muscles

There are three types of muscle tissue:

- cardiac muscle of a very special type found only in the heart
- smooth muscle found in the walls of the hollow organs of the body such as the digestive tract, the uterus and the bladder
- skeletal muscle which forms the horse's flesh and moves the horse's bones to enable him to move

From the point of view of this book, we need to consider only skeletal muscle. This is very high in protein which is why it forms a concentrated diet for carnivores. Its development and health maintenance is crucial to athletic animals like horses. Its condition can be adapted according to the horse's work, as during a fitness programme or during a period of let-down and rest.

Skeletal muscle is generously supplied with blood and nerves and, again, causes a good deal of pain when it is injured. It also, from the point of view of athleticism and bodywork, has the unfortunate quality of going into spasm and 'knotting up' when injured and remaining in that state until released by massage or other therapy. Muscles can remain in spasm for years causing long term changes in the horse's mobility, nerve damage and reduced performance ability.

Muscles need energy to be able to move and this is produced in a chemical reaction in which glucose (obtained from the food and delivered by the blood) is 'burned up' in the presence of oxygen (picked up by the blood circulating through the lungs and delivered by the blood), the end result being energy with the waste product being carbon dioxide. Muscles can store glucose (as glycogen) and oxygen (as myoglobin) for use when needed. Bear in mind that every tiny movement of the muscles needs energy, even when the horse is asleep.

If the muscles are working harder and using up supplies quicker than they can be replaced, the toxic waste product lactic acid is produced. This can cause pain in the muscles, is the cause of fatigue (combined with lack of fuel) and can damage the muscle cells. These conditions can also occur when muscles are working in an unnatural or unaccustomed way such as balancing the horse during transport, working too hard for their state of fitness, when the horse is moving differently so as to avoid causing pain to other muscles (compensatory movement) or, for instance, when the feet are uncomfortable or he is avoiding the feeling of an uncomfortable or painful saddle or bit. Bad riding can also cause them as the horse may be compelled to move in a 'forced', difficult way and probably try to compensate for how the rider is making him move. Pair driving horses frequently develop the knack of leaning into or away from the pole for the same reason.

Waste products are removed from muscles by the circulation of blood and lymph which can be assisted by correct post-work exercise and massage.

Muscles often work in specific groups in a complementary way and are controlled by the nervous system. 'Sensory' nerves are responsible for sensing or feeling what is going on in the muscle and 'motor' nerves for moving the muscle. If a horse rubs against something sharp or experiences a dig in the ribs from a rider's spur, feels the driver's whip or a kick from another horse, the sensory nerves pass a message to the central nervous system (the spinal cord and brain) to tell it what is happening. The system then passes a message back down the motor nerves to tell them to move the muscles away from the feeling or stimulus. The horse can over-ride this message and decide to disobey the human but will usually move away from a barbed wire fence or a kicking companion.

Muscle tissue is made up of long fibres (which are the muscle cells). Within each muscle fibre are small myofibrils (myo = muscle) arranged in bundles. The muscle fibres themselves are also arranged in bundles which are, in their turn, bound into larger bundles by fibrous 'connective' tissue.

There is much emphasis these days on getting muscles to stretch. In fact, muscles cannot stretch themselves but can only contract (shorten or hold themselves in 'tone'). They can only *be* stretched by the contraction, opposing them, of opposite muscle groups. It is an extremely fine inter-play between muscles to provide just the right amount of opposition to other muscles or contraction within themselves to create the movement decided upon by the horse.

Nutrition and work play a great part in enabling muscles to respond to stress or demands and grow in size and strength but maintaining a healthy environment within and around the muscles can be influenced by helping the horse to get over the results of hard work, illness or injury by means of appropriate bodywork.

There are different types of muscle fibres according to the type of work a horse is naturally best suited to do. Aerobic fibres which need a generous supply of oxygen to work will be suited to long-distance work such as hunting, steeplechasing, eventing, endurance riding, long hacks, pleasure rides and so on. Anaerobic fibres can work with little or no oxygen short-term and a predominance of these will make the horse suited to sprinting, polo, show jumping speed classes, gymkhana, reining and the like. The type of work a horse is asked to do can modify the main type of muscle fibre to some extent although, to give an extreme example, you will never change a draught horse into a racehorse.

Tendons

Muscles are attached to bones by means of modified connective and muscle tissue known as tendon. Tendon tissue is very slightly elastic due to having a 'crimped' structure which straightens out under pressure and recoils (known as 'elastic recoil') when the pressure is removed. The muscle will be attached to generally one bone at one end (called its 'origin') and to another at the other end (called its 'insertion') and there will be a joint between them. The tendon tissue at the origin is usually much shorter than that at the insertion.

A simplified example might be the leg muscles. (Horses have muscle only in the upper parts of their legs.) The muscles may attach to the forearm or upper arm or to the second thigh/gaskin or thigh bone, say, by means of short lengths of tendon tissue (at the origin) and to the lower parts of the legs and feet via longer tendons (at the insertion) with one or more joints in between such as the knee, hock or pastern joints.

To create movement, the nerve impulses or messages arrive at the muscle fibres, the myofibrils in the fibres respond by shortening or contracting to shorten the muscle and cause it to pull on the tendon at the point of insertion. The joint flexes or bends and the bone on which the tendon inserts has to move. Opposing muscles work in the same way to bring the leg back again as the first set relaxes. Whichever group of muscles is in opposition maintains a slight tension, or contraction without shortening, – muscular 'tone' – to balance or counteract the movement of its partner group, a facility which normally prevents over-extension of the joints, so helping to avoid injury.

When pressure/weight is experienced by the tendon, its crimped structure is straightened out as, for instance when weight is borne on a leg. As the weight is removed again, the crimped structure returns in the elastic recoil process. This gives the horse an energy-free boost to his stride and creates the 'spring in his step'. As horses, humans, dogs or any animal age, their tissues lose their suppleness and elasticity. Muscles in a young horse are about sixty per cent water but this figure lowers in an older animal. The tendons to some extent lose their elastic-recoil ability and the horse feels 'flatter' and 'harder' to ride (not in the sense of more difficult).

BLOOD

Very few parts of the body have no blood supply, hoof horn and the cornea of the eye being two of them. Blood is crucial to life as it carries nutrients, including water, all around the body for immediate use or for storage in the liver, muscles and other storage depots around the body: it also takes away debris such as dead and damaged cells and toxins, either taken into the body or created during metabolism as a car creates exhaust fumes. Metabolism is the sum (total) of the physical and chemical processes of life. Hormones and, for example, medicinal drugs are also carried in the blood.

Blood is a liquid organ comprising three main components – plasma, red and white cells, and platelets.

Plasma
This is made up of *serum* and *fibrinogen*. Serum is the clear, straw-coloured fluid which is the basis of blood and is ninety-two per cent water, the rest being substances dissolved in it, mainly nutrients. Fibrinogen is a protein important to the blood clotting process, so helping to repair injuries.

Cells
These are divided into *red cells* and *white cells*. The red cells are capable of picking up and carrying oxygen around the body. The white cells are of five types and help remove dead and damaged tissue and also fight and dispose of alien or injurious bacteria and viruses, being a crucial part of the immune system.

Platelets

These congregate at injury sites and work with fibrinogen to clot blood, so helping deal with haemorrhage and act as 'first aid' while new body tissue is formed and injuries are repaired. Scabs on surface injuries are made of fibrinogen and platelets and similar, softer clots form internally for the same reason.

The heart is a hollow organ which pumps the blood around the body and there are two networks of vessels leading to and from it and passing through the body's tissues and organs – arteries and veins. Arteries carry blood away from the heart and veins carry it towards the heart, a process known as venous return which is greatly aided by exercise and massage. Exercise not only encourages circulation because it makes the heart pump faster but squeezes and releases the veins through the movement of tissues, not least muscles. Massage serves the same purpose.

The heart pumps blood to the lungs where it exchanges carbon dioxide (a waste product picked up on its journey round the body) for oxygen. The oxygen is subsequently delivered all around the body.

Arteries have strong, muscular walls to help them cope with the pressure or force of the blood sent through them by the heart; they also have a recoil mechanism which keeps pushing the blood along through them. The walls of veins are thinner as by the time the blood reaches them on its way back to the heart and lungs, the force has lessened considerably. Some veins have valves in them to stop the backflow of blood. Both arteries and veins gradually become smaller and finer, eventually meshing in a very complex and copious network of microscopic vessels having walls only one cell thick, called the capillary network. Substances pass both ways through the capillary walls to and from the tissues – a process without which life could not continue.

LYMPH

Lymph is another of the body's fluids and helps with fighting disease, draining excess fluid in tissues and the blood (so helping to maintain the body's fluid balance) and acts to 'cleanse' and feed tissues with no blood supply, including joint cartilage.

It has its own system of channels but no heart or other pumping mechanism and no valves in the channels: therefore, exercise with its movement and pressure of tissue surrounding the channels is essential to help prevent lymph accumulating in, especially, the limbs but also other tissues. Again, massage and general bodywork can help with this process.

The lymphatic system has many nodes or glands whose job is to deactivate bacteria and viruses filtered from lymph passing through them. There are many glands but we mainly think of lymph glands as those in the throat, in front of the shoulder and in the groin. If the glands become hot and swollen as, for instance, in strangles, we can feel and even see them easily as they work overtime to cope with disease, producing antibodies and filtering out germs and damaged tissue.

Lymphangitis is a painful condition in which both or, more usually, one hind leg (although it can be a front leg) swells and becomes hot and hard. It can be caused by infection but also by injury which may block or damage lymph channels. A common cause of one type of lymphangitis is too much food and not enough exercise. Fluid escapes through the walls of weakened or damaged blood and lymph vessels into the surrounding tissues where it becomes trapped, causing a 'filled' leg which pits on pressure – i.e. when you press the area with your finger the depression remains for a little while.

FEET

What have feet to do with bodywork? Surely you can't massage horses' feet. In a way, you can. The coronet bands and heel areas not only consist of soft tissue but contain pressure points used in shiatsu and acupressure which are dealt with briefly in this book. Reflexology is applied from the hock and knee downwards (equivalent to the human ankle and wrist respectively), the hoof corresponding to the human middle toe or finger nails.

The other vital element as regards the effect feet have on the functioning of the horse's body is their balance and comfort. Feet with problems invariably cause problems elsewhere in the horse's body, often in the back as the horse tries to alter his body balance and weight distribution (which can only be achieved and controlled by the use of his muscles) to relieve the discomfort or even pain in anything from one to all four feet. If you have ever had a foot or ankle injury, you may remember how you felt its 'offshoot' effects in the muscles of your back as you tried to adjust your weight away from your injury, with or without the help of a walking stick or crutches.

The muscles used are, also, often not those used in normal movement: they are muscles the horse may not be accustomed to using much when moving correctly and, being 'unfit' are ill-suited to their new job of weight adjustment.

Feet are very individual things and farriery is a great skill which many horseowners may not yet fully appreciate. If you are fortunate enough to have a good farrier who has the time and inclination to really explain your horse's feet to you and why he shoes him the way he does, you will learn a very great deal. The knock-on effects on your horse's body, action, comfort and performance can be tremendous. You can call in all the bodywork experts you like to work on that mysterious back injury or apparent quarter or shoulder lameness, but if the feet are not put right nothing else can be, either.

There are various ways of shoeing horses, full discussions of which are outside the scope of this book but some mention should be made. The traditional way of shoeing horses with metal shoes has stood the test of many centuries. Now other schools of thought are gaining prominence and many people are keeping their horses without shoes with varying levels of success in terms of comfort for the horse. Sadly, some have a real 'bee in their bonnet' about this matter and I find that many horses are going barefoot who, to me, really seem to need shoes. Others do very well without shoes and their feet appear to be bigger, well balanced with expert trimming and, it seems, better blood circulation in the feet because they are not constricted by horseshoe nails. Horses do need time and well-balanced feeding to develop feet strong enough to go barefoot and to accustom themselves to the very different feel they will experience without shoes. Some never adapt but others become more sure-footed and free-moving. It is a very individual thing and definitely a topic for discussion with your farrier.

There are different types of trim, too, for the feet. Horses on all but soft ground naturally appear to wear their toes square or straight across the toe and I had a farrier many years ago who trimmed and shod my horse this way because, he said, 'it's more natural'. The horse certainly went better than when more conventionally shod.

There is also the four-point trim which leaves the horse with four main points of contact (with the ground) in his feet – two at the front of the quarters (sides) and two nearer the heels, plus the frog, of course. Again, the basis of this is that it is a more natural wear pattern. It takes a good deal of skill to both trim *and shoe* a horse this way and many farriers disagree with the method, in any case.

Structure

The horn of the hoof is insensitive like our fingernails but underneath the horn are very sensitive, complex structures which are relatively easily bruised, stressed and torn. The basis for the shape of the foot is the pedal (foot) bone which is crescent-shaped and fairly round in the fore feet but more oval in the hind. The short pastern bone is partway inside the horny hoof capsule and partway above the coronet. It forms a two-way joint inside the hoof with the pedal bone and the navicular bone and, in the pastern, with the bottom of the long pastern bone. The top of the long pastern bone forms the fetlock joint, with the addition of two small sesamoid bones behind it.

The navicular bone is also a type of sesamoid bone: sesamoid bones act as pulleys to lessen friction on the tendons running over them.

The coronet band at the top of the wall is similar to our cuticle and is where the horn is produced to form the protective horny casing or capsule to house the tendons, ligaments, blood vessels, nerves and other structures inside the hoof. It can take a year for horn at the toe to grow down from coronet to ground which is why hoof problems and their resulting effects on the legs and body can take some time to rectify.

Immediately inside the horny wall and on the surface of the pedal bone is a system of firmly interlocking leaves of tissue (the laminae) which suspend the foot inside its casing so the horse is actually slung inside his feet, not standing on them. If the connection between these laminae is weakened as in laminitis, the pedal bone can come away from its bond with the inside of the horny wall and move downwards, sometimes even to the extent that the toe of the bone comes through the sole. Obviously, this condition is excruciatingly painful for the horse.

The bones of the feet can also suffer from osteoarthritic conditions, often due to foot imbalance, poor nutrition, concussion or bad shoeing.

Underneath the foot on the outside can be seen the sole, the slightly arched area of thin horn between the weight-bearing rim or ground surface of the wall and the triangular-shaped frog, which looks and feels like a wedge of India rubber. The frog gives the horse some security in movement provided it can touch the ground (which it cannot in a shod foot on hard ground) and is part of the 'pumping' mechanism of the foot which sends the copious blood round the foot.

The demarcation line between the bearing surface of the wall and the sole is called the white line because that is exactly what it is and marks the line of the laminae going up inside the foot. The farrier normally keeps his nails in the wall horn to avoid injury to the foot.

Inside the foot at the heel is a firm, spongy pad of fibrous tissue called the digital cushion. Extending upwards from the ends of the pedal bone are the lateral cartilages. They can just be felt at the sides of the pastern above the coronet bone and give the back of the hoof, where most expansion takes place during weight-bearing, some stability.

Function

Ideas of exactly how the horse's foot works have been thrown about over the centuries and still are being. One current school of thought, based on scientific research in the United States of America, believes that because horses' feet land (or should land) heels first, the general expansion of the foot, mainly in its back half, sucks blood into the back of the foot, dissipating the concussive force, sending the blood up the leg and allowing fresh blood to replace it as weight is removed.

Horses undoubtedly evolved to go on grassland and certainly go better on old turf than anything else. This comprises soil and an established cushion of grass roots providing both absorption (but not too much) and spring. Soft ground can cause excessive stretching forces on the soft tissues in the leg and stress on the ligaments, muscles and their related tendons as the horse tries to pull his leg up out of the ground whether it be mud or soft, dry sand (many outdoor manèges are too deep today and create such problems). Conversely, hard ground (such as zebras and donkeys evolved to live on) can cause internal foot problems through concussion such as bruising and resulting inflammation in the feet, and not least laminitis.

All these things can cause muscular and other soft tissue problems further up the leg and in the body as a whole due to compensatory movement on the part of the horse. Foot health, nutrition and balance, whether the horse is shod or not, are vital to a comfortable horse able to move naturally and effectively.

SECTION 2

INJURY AND HEALING

The main problem with treating horses or any animals is, of course, that they often do not complain about pain. Some horses *are* more sensitive to pain than others, but some make matters worse for themselves by stoically keeping on and doing their best under adverse and often worsening circumstances. Another major problem is that the horse cannot tell us exactly where the pain is, just how bad or slight it is or exactly what kind of discomfort or pain it is.

Normally, therefore, it is up to the horse's human connections to decide whether or not he is in pain (because most injuries involve pain to some degree as we all know), where the pain is, why this might have occurred and what to do about it.

When pain is not spotted or even suspected, the horse's work programme will probably continue as normal and the injury may become worse (in which case it should become obvious) or may, indeed, lessen if slight as the body's natural healing processes come into play whether or not the horse is working. Often, the horse starts moving with what we call 'compensatory action' which means that he starts using his body differently from what is natural to him in order to avoid the pain. He will move so that the injured part carries as little weight as possible and moves as little as possible. This is the body's natural reaction to pain in order to free the part from stress and prevent further injury to it.

Unfortunately, when muscles not normally used for a particular movement are brought into play, they themselves and their associated tissues such as tendons, in particular, ligaments and adjacent soft tissues become overstressed due to the unaccustomed demands on them and can either develop abnormally or become injured, too. This becomes a vicious cycle because the horse's action may be affected to the extent that he, say, does not move true and may start interfering (brushing, speedicutting, over-reaching etc). The muscles in one area, one side of his back let's say, become much more developed because of this new use of them, so his development becomes lopsided and uneven. This can adversely affect the fit of his saddle which may have been good when his muscle development was normal but which may start to hurt him through uneven pressure, shifting, twisting or pinching now that he has changed shape.

OPPOSITE: *There are many aspects of healing and health maintenance. A good part of the process is the relationship between horse and human and the will or intent of the healer. As with humans, horses and all animals respond to love, care and kindness tempered by knowledge and knowing when to call in the right kind of help*

This in itself can cause more injury to the back. Once again the horse compensates for it and so it goes on. This may sound like an exaggeration but this is how the cycle of undetected and untreated injury and pain goes on. The horse may eventually become unrideable because his body is in such a bad condition. At least he may become more difficult to ride. The owner becomes perplexed about his deterioration and may turn him out for a rest which will probably do nothing to put matters right, just relax him a little and reduce his fitness. When the horse is brought back into work, it all begins again.

An experienced professional should be able to spot the problem with a good idea of what is wrong, depending on his or her speciality, for example a teacher with knowledge and experience of anatomy and action, a good farrier who not only studies the wear pattern on the horse's shoes but also the way he moves and is shaped, a veterinary surgeon certainly, a physiotherapist or a massage therapist likewise, a trained/qualified saddle *fitter* and so on.

Unfortunately for owners, we are often so close to our horses and see them all the time that we do not always notice minor changes occurring very slowly, even if the horse's performance is changing. It is very well worthwhile to give your horse as objective a look-over as possible at least once a week as if he were someone else's horse and keep notes of your observations, muscle development, action and so on.

SIGNS OF PAIN

The most obvious signs of discomfort and pain are:

- obvious, if slight, lameness
- deterioration in performance
- development of napping, or refusing to work
- playing up
- the horse starting to go crookedly
- the horse starting to have trouble lying down and getting up
- the horse objecting when tacked up or having rugs put on
- heart rate/pulse slow to return to normal despite the horse's being fit (an increased heart rate being indicative of pain)
- deterioration in temperament
- change in attitude to life – more sensitive or dull and resigned
- groaning and/or patchy sweating which are signs of significant, severe pain

ACUTE (SUDDEN OR VERY RECENT) INJURY

When injury occurs to muscle or soft tissue, the cells making up that tissue are ruptured and damaged. Fluid escapes from the cells into the surrounding area, and if blood and lymph capillaries or vessels are torn and ruptured these fluids, too, will seep out and congregate in the area, causing congestion.

The classic reaction to injury is inflammation which combines pain, swelling and heat. The pain comes with pressure on the nerve endings which tell the central nervous system that an injury has occurred, the swelling occurs due to escaped fluid but also because the body's reaction is to send more blood and lymph to an already congested area, and the heat occurs due to the excess, heat-carrying blood brought to the area.

The inflammation can be so bad and the area so congested that helpful circulation through it (bringing oxygen and nutrients for repair and removing dead and damaged tissues and toxins) is significantly hampered. This is why, although inflammation is a natural reaction, it is usual to try to reduce it with cold treatments of various sorts and anti-inflammatory drugs for at least the first forty-eight hours after an injury after which, if it has subsided sufficiently, other treatments can be started according to veterinary advice, specifically physiotherapy in many cases. Obviously, the length of time over which the injury progresses will depend on its type and severity and how quickly first aid (often in the form of immobilisation, drug administration and possibly cold packs) is given.

The horse may certainly need to be box-rested for anything from days to months depending on the severity of the injury. This is a time when a conscientious and sensible owner can help the horse to endure a very boring and possibly frustrating period by means of correct diet, bodywork such as appropriate massage, shiatsu, grooming and wisping, aromatherapy and so on. With sensitive treatment, it is surprising how well many animals adapt to box rest.

The healing process can take many months in the case of seriously injured tendon and ligament tissue which are naturally poorly supplied with blood. Muscle tissue heals quicker because of its excellent blood supply. After the period of box rest, it may or may not be decided to turn the horse out to recuperate.

Evolution is an ongoing process and perfection has not yet been reached. This is why, left to itself, the body will certainly heal after a fashion, sometimes very well, but we can help it along and often end up with better results than if nature were left to herself.

Blood and lymph between them bring oxygen and nutrients to the area from which the body can make new tissue and carry away dead and damaged cells for disposal. They try also to drain the area of excess fluid clearing the way for normal circulation to be restored, so speeding both the clearing-up process and the creation of new tissue.

As soft tissue (muscle, tendon, ligament, connective tissue or fascia) begins to heal, tissues can literally 'stick' or adhere to each other as new tissue is being made, and two surfaces which are normally separate can become connected. This new, repair tissue is called scar tissue (it is fibrous and less sensitive and also weaker than the original tissue) and the unions between tissues are called adhesions. A substance in the blood called fibrinogen helps to clot blood and so prevent bleeding and this can also stick to the surface of surrounding tissues. The downside of adhesions is that they can tear when the horse starts moving again, so creating a new injury and the process starts again.

Physiotherapy machines expertly used, hot and cold treatments, massage and very gentle manipulations of injured parts such as flexing, stretching and circling of limbs, depending on the injury, can all help to prevent adhesions forming. Gradually, short walks of five to ten minutes in hand can be started. The object of these gentle and careful movements is to break down the adhesions before they become fully formed, so greatly reducing the likelihood of re-injury which often used to occur in previous times when horses with soft-tissue injuries were box-rested with no exercise at all for much longer than they may be today.

A general plan of action in the case of soft tissue injury, depending always on the advice of the veterinary surgeon and possibly the referred physiotherapist, may be:

1. Box rest the horse (normally with constant fibre – hay/haylage – and water) and relieve pain, congestion and blockages in the injured area. This may be achieved by means of anti-inflammatory drugs which will reduce pain and inflammation, analgesics (pain killers), hot and cold treatments and gentle massage of the area around the injury.

2. As soon as the horse can tolerate it and the inflammation has subsided sufficiently, very gently start moving the area, unless immobilisation has to be maintained, by means of slight and simple flexing and stretching exercises, also continuing with the gentle massage.
3. When ready, start five- to ten-minute walks in hand, say just around the stable yard or up and down the drive, two or three times a day, to keep the part moving. This will also help to relieve the horse's monotony and at first the horse may be quite lively in hand so use headgear which will offer adequate control, probably not just an ordinary headcollar. Increase the length of the walks as advised by the vet and physiotherapist, if the latter is involved.

After the walking-in-hand stage of the recovery, walking under saddle can be started and the horse gradually rehabilitated by various means discussed in this book. The owner will certainly play a crucial part in this rehabilitation by not only obeying the vet's instructions to the letter but also taking things a step further by being prepared to use professional physiotherapy plus supplementary treatments such as bodywork techniques suitable for owner application.

With expert care during and after injury as rehabilitation progresses, it is possible these days to restore an injured area to, or very nearly to, the level of strength and function it enjoyed before the injury. The problem with scar tissue is that it is fibrous and weaker than the original tissue and does not have the same function. Therefore, if the horse is returned to the same level of work the same part may re-injure more easily. That fact plus the development of adhesions often led, in the past, to disappointing levels of healing. Today, however, physiotherapy, stretching and massage can greatly improve this situation.

CHRONIC INJURY (PRESENT FOR SOME TIME)

If acute injuries are not spotted and treated, the problem can become chronic (longer lasting). The initial inflammation will die down but one of the body's ways of protecting itself may come into play – the muscles may go into spasm. Muscles may remain tight after work or be very slightly overstressed and if not eased and relieved by massage and stretching may actually go into spasm. Muscle spasms are tight, hard, constant contractions of muscles which stay shortened or contracted – in spasm – without the horse consciously 'instructing' his muscles to contract.

When a part of the body is painful, the muscles around it often tighten up to prevent further movement of the part and so protect it from further injury by preventing its full use. Muscles in spasm can then themselves become painful and, in effect, injured. Blood and lymph cannot circulate effectively through tight, hardened tissue which is squeezing the vessels, so the tissues do not receive their necessary quota of nutrients, oxygen and waste removal. These areas can become bigger and bigger as surrounding tissues act to protect those they perceive as being injured, and this state can last for weeks, months even years. The horse may be in more or less discomfort, stiffness or pain all this time but work round it by means of compensatory movement.

These situations can all be prevented and relieved by means of careful stretching and massage.

Trigger points are small, painful areas of injured muscle tissue. They are areas of toxin (lactic acid) accumulation due to inefficient oxygen delivery and waste removal and are both hard and very tender. They can cause what is called 'referred pain' or pain due to nerve compression at some point distant from the actual trigger point, depending on which area the compressed nerve serves. Because the muscle does not relax fully due to the painful spot, it may create tension at its point of insertion on to a bone and the joint between that bone and the one on which the muscle inserts will not function correctly because it cannot go through its full range of movement. This can lead to joint inflammation and pain which may be treated – but the real problem lies elsewhere.

A professional therapist may treat spasm and trigger points with deep massage and acupuncture but there is a great deal an owner can do by means of massaging the more superficial muscles, stretching exercises, shiatsu and possibly acupressure.

Muscle spasm and trigger points can both be caused by

- trauma to the muscles – direct injury
- too high a demand on the muscle for its strength
- fatigue and overwork in general
- incorrect work where the rider keeps the horse 'on the bit' or collected for too long a period without adequate breaks, during schooling or work, of allowing the horse to stretch *fully*

On the latter point, these essential breaks involve sitting lightly and putting the buckle end of the reins on the horse's withers and allowing or asking him to stretch his head and neck right down to the ground for one or two circuits of the school. Even standing still and encouraging him to drop his head is a relief but it is amazing the number of riders who are reluctant to do this.

A long rein is not the same as a loose or free rein and horses do not stretch freely (involving the head, neck *and* back) on a rein which is merely long as opposed to completely loose. Many reins are not long enough to permit this and I frequently advise new clients to buy some longer reins or have their present ones extended so that the horse may be worked correctly and encouraged to fully stretch and relax in between spells of work – a manoeuvre which is so crucial to blood circulation and, therefore, muscle health.

Your reins should be long enough to enable you to sit upright in the saddle with your elbows back at your hips and your hands on the pommel whilst the horse stretches his head right down to the ground with no tension at all on the reins.

INJURIES CAUSED BY ILL-FITTING TACK

Saddles

As we learn more and more about saddle fitting and suitability (at least compared with previous generations, it seems), we realise what a minefield can be the task of finding a saddle which fits both horse and rider, and it makes us wonder just how many problems and injuries of yesteryear were caused by saddles which simply did not fit but we never realised it.

Today, we are fortunate to have a new breed of expert to help – the trained and qualified saddle fitter. Different countries may have their own training courses and qualifications in this field – in the UK The British Equestrian Trade Association and The Worshipful Company of Saddlers both run training courses in saddle fitting.

Master saddlers have immense skill in saddle design and making. It is a true craft which is thousands of years old and is still developing. They obviously study anatomy and physiology to understand how the horse moves and how his back works. They are asked to supply saddles for backs of all kinds not to mention driving pads and collars and a good saddler can come up with solutions for many problems.

The new field of saddle fitting, its training and qualification system can only enhance the superb saddles which are now available. Unfortunately, many tack shops and stores still do not have qualified saddle fitters but the situation is improving. I would certainly advise readers to ask, in whatever retail outlet they are considering, if they have a qualified saddle fitter on the staff and have him or her fit your saddle to your horse and yourself. There are people in the industry who have been supplying and fitting saddles for many years and have the competence of experience and sensitivity for horses, but if you are in any doubt use a shop which can offer a qualified saddle fitter and you should be assured of getting a saddle and girth which really fit your horse and which will not, therefore, injure him.

Bridles

Bridles are made by saddlers and bits and stirrups are made by loriners. A reputable book on tack, its types, designs and fit, will help you to make sure that your bridle really fits your horse – not too tight around the ears, throatlatch hanging half way down the circular jawbones and the noseband sufficiently loose to not only permit the horse to breathe properly but to slightly open his mouth so that he can actually give to the bit when you ask him to do so. He cannot do this in a tight noseband so you are fighting a losing battle and more or less forcing the horse to use his muscles incorrectly by assuming a forced, false head carriage, often accompanied by a hollow back. You should be able to run a finger under all straps of your bridle and noseband, and fit your hand sideways between the throatlatch and his jaw.

The width of the bit should allow you to fit the width of one finger on one side of his mouth between the bit cheek or ring and the horse's cheek. As for bit height, the correct fit for different basic bits is as follows:

- A jointed snaffle bit should create just *one* wrinkle at the corners of the horse's mouth; otherwise it will stretch the skin there, could cause it to crack and will, in any case, be uncomfortable. This also applies to the bridoon (thin, small-ringed snaffle) of a double bridle
- My view is that a double-jointed bit such as a French link is usually more comfortable for the horse than a single-jointed bit
- An unjointed bit such as a half moon/mullen-mouthed bit or a ported bit whether snaffle, pelham or Kimblewick, should touch the corners of the mouth *without* wrinkling them
- The curb bit of a double bridle should lie about ½ inch or 1 cm below the bridoon with the latter lying on top of it in the mouth. It is quite incorrect for the curb bit of a double bridle to touch the corners of the mouth and very uncomfortable for the horse

Curb chains should lie well down in the horse's chin or curb groove, not ride part way up the lower jawbones. Lip straps, although regarded as correct, often prevent the curb chain lying correctly. Short upper bit cheeks, maybe combined with longer hooks than normal, also help the chain to lie in the correct place.

Finally, never use a noseband such as a flash or Grakle or any other noseband which goes underneath a bit with a curb chain as seems to be becoming a fashion at the time of writing. This could be said to show a serious lack of understanding of the art and science of bitting, equine psychology and equine biomechanics. A bit of this type cannot possibly work correctly when hampered by such a noseband. An ordinary cavesson noseband is the type to use in this situation.

If the saddle, girth, bridle and bit are uncomfortable the horse will be mentally stressed, as are we if wearing uncomfortable clothing or equipment, and will naturally try to move in a compensatory way to avoid the discomfort. This, as explained earlier, can result in unnatural and incorrect muscle use and ultimately in injury.

THE CONCEPT OF ENERGY IN HEALING

During the 1990s, I drifted into more of an interest in complementary, alternative, holistic therapies and modalities. My grandmother had been a healer using traditional medicines and herbs (who worked with, not in competition with, her local doctor) so I had been brought up with those concepts and treatments but knew nothing much about eastern medicine and its dependence on correcting the energy or life force which it teaches flows around the body in a twenty-four-hour cycle. I had heard various names for this force or energy – the chi of China, the qi (pronounced 'ki') of Japan, the pneuma of ancient Greece and the prana of Indian Ayurvedic medicine – but no one was able to actually pinpoint or describe it.

I saw an advertisement for a preliminary course in the Japanese therapy of shiatsu which, along with acupressure, is closely related to acupuncture, now an accepted therapy in the west. It was to be taught by an American teacher and practitioner called Pamela Hannay and I decided to enrol on this Level I Shiatsu for Horses course. I admit that I was doubtful and a bit sceptical but for some reason I still went ahead.

I found myself, having paid a few hundred pounds in advance, sitting on the floor of a village hall with a lot of strangers watching this very well-groomed, serene American lady wearing what I would call a martial arts outfit, telling us about qi (the Japanese word for what English-speaking people would probably call energy). I started to feel that this was all a bit airy-fairy, I had wasted my money, this couldn't possibly work and began to wonder why I was there.

I never said a word but Pamela looked across at me and said gently: 'You're here because you know it's for you and you will find out this week that it *does* work.' How right she was. I had read the pre-course book, tried to take in what she was saying and approached my first 'patient' with humility and doubt. I assessed him with Pamela watching and noting and agreeing with my comments, worked on him for an hour with Pamela checking on us now and then (he was having none of it at first), and then she assessed the obvious improvement in him.

I could not believe that a raw and rather sceptical beginner, *who still did not truly believe in this therapy*, had wrought such a change in a physically and mentally screwed up horse in such a short time. I knew that it wasn't me but the therapy, the 'moving of qi' round his body, the freeing of 'blockages', the strong feeling of healing intent and goodwill I had towards the horse (who was ostensibly sound and in work) – and by the end of the week I could barely wait to get home and work on my case study horses, learn all I could, study the course handouts and other books and return for my Level II course the following year which I did.

Pamela was already ill by then and told me, whilst she was giving me a shiatsu treatment as part of the course, that she had extended her 'sell-by date' as she put it considerably already through supporting her orthodox treatment with various complementary treatments. Sadly, Pamela died before she could run the Level III course the year after that – an irreplaceable loss to her husband, family, friends, students and patients human and equine.

Her enduring gift has been the promotion of shiatsu and its related therapies internationally. Because of her sensible, businesslike, generous and peaceful attitude, I am only one of many people who now know from study, observation and experience as a shiatsu practitioner that 'qi' or whatever you wish to call it exists and affects every living body. So now I have to try to explain more about it, based on my studies with and because of Pamela, to those readers of this book who may be even more sceptical than I was when I first met her.

'May The Force Be With You'

I am going to call the life force Energy because English-speaking, western readers are familiar with that word. I should also like to give, for the benefit of the doubtful, what I remember of the famous quote from *Hamlet*, to the effect that 'there are more things in Heaven and Earth, Horatio, than' and then I think it continues 'are dreamt of in your philosophy' and that is so, so true.

The attitude of 'Science' has always been that something cannot be accepted if it is not proven to work. My attitude is that just because something is not proven does not mean that it is not so. It is certainly true that many things happen in this world and in healing for which there is no explanation. The field of 'hard science' (I still believe in that, too, and am currently taking an Open University degree in Life Sciences) has frequently tried to find scientifically acceptable proof that various complementary therapies and so-called 'energy medicines' are effective or otherwise, so far without much success.

Orthodox science and medicine (as started by Newton, continued by Descartes and brought to a head by the necessities of World War II) does accept the existence if not of a life force type of energy then of chemical substances called endorphins and encephalins – the body's own opiate-like painkillers and sedatives – and other natural hormones which have a calming effect on the body. They are released during such therapies as shiatsu, acupressure and acupuncture and probably during physical exertion and trauma. It is often not until the body and mind have calmed down a little after, say, an accident or injury, that pain starts to be felt.

It is also known that healing tends to take place more easily and effectively if the sick or injured person's distress is eased and pain or other uncomfortable symptoms relieved. Endorphins do that but do not seem to actually have a healing quality themselves. Probably they pave the way for the body's immune system and energy to do the actual healing.

We all hear the word 'energy' every day – energy in the form of gas and electricity, recouping our energy after a hard day, creating more energy in our horse's way of going, running out of energy, high-energy foods and so on. No one denies that energy exists as the wind, currents in the sea and gravity exist, but they are all invisible and intangible. We can feel their *effects* but we cannot see or touch them.

Many eastern civilisations believe that all living things have an energy running through and around them which signifies that they are not only alive but sick or healthy, happy, sad, emotionally disturbed or balanced and so on. The therapies and modalities employed in these civilisations are based on restoring or maintaining a balanced, free flow of energy through the body. If the energy is disturbed in any way, blocked and excessive in one area or depleted in another, sickness ensues: the therapies' whole aim is to restore an even flow. Disturbance can be caused by physical or mental trauma, poor diet and body care, anxiety, grief, excitement and even extremes of weather.

In addition to the concept of energy, there is that of Yin and Yang or male and female –

opposites. Everything is made up of a blend of opposites. In everything male there is an element of female and in everything female there is an element of male: this also applies to dark and light, weak and strong, sweet and sour and so on. This book is not the place to go into all those aspects of eastern philosophy and therapy but there are plenty of books which do.

The body's energy flows around the body in channels or meridians (the number of which varies according to the exact therapy you are considering) and the concept of whether or not these physically or anatomically exist is also a point of contention between western and eastern medicine. The meridians may run just under the skin or deep within the body, some being accessible by touch and others only by stretching and manipulating the body. They are often said to exist in grooves in the body, such as between muscles and organs, like a valley between hills. Personally, I have never heard or read that they are, for instance, physical tubes like blood or lymph vessels or wires which convey invisible electricity (the existence of which, again, no one doubts).

My feeling and intuition is that the meridians and channels are *directions* like the direction of the wind or a current in the sea. A north-easterly wind, for example, may undoubtedly be blowing from the north east; it is not contained within a tube but it is certainly there. Sailors come to know the stable currents in the seas and rivers they sail habitually. They are reliably present to be used or avoided, but are certainly not contained inside anything physical.

If you think of energy and energy meridians in this way the concept of eastern healing will be much easier for you to grasp and if you can also accept that there are, indeed, more things in Heaven and Earth than we have ever dreamed of, perhaps this similarly will help you to accept that energy healing can certainly work – *if the intent of the therapist truly is to heal and help*.

That statement seems to be at the crux of the matter, and rather ephemeral for those inexperienced in energy medicine. No matter what touching form of energy medicine you choose or believe in, if you honestly want to heal your horse, your dog, your child, your partner or whoever else, it can work. I find, though, that as I am drawn to shiatsu I need to keep to its teachings, its meridians, its philosophy and its principles and then I *am* almost always able to make a difference.

That word 'almost' is not a get-out. No therapy or medicine, orthodox, complementary or alternative, works for everyone every time. When using touch therapies or bodywork on your horse, be sensitive to what you feel comfortable with and what seems to 'fit' with your horse, what suits him and what seems to help him, then you should surely be able to enhance his quality of life, health and well-being.

The therapist in such techniques is the medium through whom healing energies pass from the environment. The therapist may simply hold his or her hands over the horse or may touch or manipulate him in a more structured way according to the therapy. Every time we stroke our horse, groom him, rub him down, school him well, exercise him, put a saddle on or do anything significantly physical to him, we are working a meridian somewhere or an acupressure point. These points are energy 'openings', mainly on meridians, where the animal's energy is particularly close to the surface, accessible and susceptible to pressure.

A well-groomed, well-exercised and correctly schooled horse – all else being equal – looks glowing with health, not least because the regular physical contact and the movement of his body are 'working' on his meridians either by direct pressure (maybe unknown to the owner) or due to being stretched and 'worked' by his body movements. Massage therapists and physiotherapists, not to mention osteopaths and chiropractors, are also operating meridians even if they do not believe in or know about them.

It all comes back to the matter of intent: such people are usually concerned for the health and well-being of the horse and this is conveyed through their touch. Horses which are 'used' but not particularly cared for may shine superficially and do their job, but they do not have that bloom of love about them which comes from truly caring attention of whatever kind.

Here's to the future

To close this section, I find it interesting to note from personal experience and from talking to friends in the medical profession that many nurses and auxiliary health workers from different cultural backgrounds, eastern and western, are trained and qualified practitioners of one or more complementary therapies including those involving bodywork and I believe that a few doctors are, too, if not many. Some therapies such as acupuncture and homoeopathy are available on the UK National Health Service.

As for veterinary surgeons, the concept of separating animal from human medicine seems to be a western one, but some veterinary surgeons are also homoeopathic veterinary surgeons and a very few are also qualified herbalists. These latter two modalities do not come under the heading of bodywork as it is discussed in this book. It would be interesting to know if there are any vets who are also qualified massage therapists, physiotherapists or osteopaths, for example. It would also be interesting to know how many veterinary nurses are trained and qualified complementary therapists, like their counterparts in human medicine.

Interestingly, few vets seem to refuse an owner a referral to a complementary therapist if requested. Even the very cynical ones with 'atheist' views agree to it if the client wants to 'waste his or her money', backed up by the attitude that when the therapist makes a mess of things the vet will be called in to clear up the mess anyway. Most vets are more forward-thinking than this and agree, some are open-minded and agree and some are in favour of such therapies and actually recommend them to owners but haven't the time or inclination to take time off from a busy practice to train themselves.

In the UK now we have a fascinating multi-racial society with third and fourth generation people of eastern origins who retain their ancestral cultures, religions and systems of healing. Such societies also exist in, for example, the United States of America and they also have Native American healing systems and access to South American beliefs and healing systems, too, which we hardly have here. Ancient systems are clearly of much more ancient lineage than conventional western orthodox medicine which is continuing to develop but which, in its present form, is little over sixty years old. Prior to taking its current form, doctors relied on older remedies of organic (mainly plant) and inorganic origin. Modern painkillers, synthetic drugs and, most of all, antibiotics, changed all that.

I think that all this goes to show that, more than ever, the different medical and healing schools of thought are slowly coming together and can be used side by side for the benefit of all under the multi-disciplinary umbrella of Healing.

SECTION 3

MANAGEMENT AND CARE TECHNIQUES

GROOMING

How often have you turned up at the stables, grabbed your grooming kit, given your horse a quick quarter over, tacked up and gone out on exercise, partly because you want to ride and partly because you have to 'get the horse out'? This will particularly be the case if you are one of the unfortunate many who have to keep their horses at livery yards which offer little or no decent winter turnout.

Grooming is often regarded as one of those time-consuming chores which have to be done on show days (although a good shampooing is quicker and less tiring than a thorough grooming but not, in the author's opinion, anything like so effective or beneficial) but for the rest of the time many horses live on a lick and a promise. Grooming properly is hard work and a fit, experienced groom does well to do one horse in half an hour.

However, grooming properly and thoroughly in an unrushed, perceptive and caring way is a greatly under-valued technique today. Many owners who have not had the benefit of spending a lot of time in a well-run professional yard (and not all professional yards are well-run by any means, believe it or not) have never been able to absorb the meticulous stable management policies and techniques, old and modern, which are *de rigeur* in such establishments and which are the backbone and foundation on which the horses' well-being is based.

Full, thorough and normally daily grooming of horses in work is one of these techniques. This book is not a horse care (or training) manual and every little technique of grooming is not going to be covered, but it is going to explain the right attitude to grooming, its benefits and the techniques of good body brushing followed (see the next section) by wisping, or banging as it is sometimes known, which will be an eye-opener to many younger owners. The two processes together – thorough grooming incorporating body-brushing, plus wisping – are known as 'strapping' which sounds cruel and about the origins of which word I haven't the foggiest!

Correct body brushing alone is almost as good as a massage and combined with wisping it is hard to beat. A good strapping, like this, takes an hour and would do every bit as much for the owner's fitness as an expensive and time-consuming trip to the gym, plus spending time with and building up a rapport with your horse. I am sure it would be worth cancelling your gym subscription and getting physical with your horse instead. It would be much more enjoyable for both of you, plus you get the brilliant end result of a glossy, muscled-up horse who feels and looks fabulous and a fit, strong you.

The best tools for the job

Proper grooming of a horse is certainly a form of massage and, like massage, can be stimulating or relaxing. The usual basic grooming kit is familiar – hoof pick for removing dirt from the feet; dandy brush for removing dried sweat, mud and 'stable stains', i.e. dried on droppings and urine; body brush for removing grease and dust from a short coat (it is less effective on a long coat); metal curry comb to clean the body brush; and water brush for 'laying' or flattening the forelock, mane and tail hair, used damp.

There are all sorts of additions such as plastic-toothed or rubber, ridged curry 'combs' for helping remove caked-on mud, rough cactus cloths for removing superficial dirt, hoof dressings, (ordinary hoof oils are not normally a good idea as they can interfere with the hoof's moisture balance), coat dressings of various kinds to add a sheen and aid the removal of dirt, sweat scrapers to remove sweat and water although you can use the sides of your hands, and various other inventions which may or may not be helpful.

For effectiveness, the best brushes are certainly those of natural bristle. Synthetic ones just do not do the job properly in my experience. They do not remove dirt so effectively and what they do remove tends to stick to the bristles – synthetic bristles do not shed dirt as well as natural ones. Synthetic bristles are surely not so comfortable on the horse's skin as natural ones and their ends tend to split and hold hairs and bedding in the same way that a synthetic yard brush splits and builds up bedding on the bristles, quickly becoming more or less useless.

If you want your grooming to be an art and a massage-like benefit to your horse, shop and telephone around and buy the best natural bristle brushes you can find. They will last longer than synthetic ones, too. If you are told, 'no one makes them any more' don't believe it because it isn't true. The better and more traditional saddlers will either stock or acquire them for you. Insist and ring or shop around till you get what you want.

Dandy brushes will have a wooden back and longish, coarse, stiff bristles. (When they are worn out you can use them for scrubbing out buckets and mangers.)

Body brushes will have finer, shorter, denser and softer bristles, but if they are too soft they won't get through the coat to the skin. They need some spring and resilience in them and need to be densely packed together. Another important and helpful refinement is to get a body brush with a real *leather* back. These mould to your hand like nothing else and, in time, become part of it, making your job so much easier and your work so much more effective.

Your brushes should be washed occasionally. The traditional way of doing this is to 'dap' the bristles only up and down in a strong, hot solution of washing soda water in a metal tray (wearing strong rubber or plastic gloves to guard against splashes) which is still available from ironmongers and a few supermarkets. Do not let the solution reach the very tops of the bristles or the back of the brush as it is caustic. After the grease has been removed, dip the bristles only, again, in strong, salty water to reharden them. Do not rinse off the salt. Shake the brush downwards to remove excess water and stand the brush bristles down to dry off naturally. Clean leather backs as for bridle leather.

This may all sound like a lot of fuss but it makes all the difference to the effectiveness of your grooming tools. If you don't fancy using soda, use hot water and washing up liquid in the same way, and follow up with the salty water.

Quartering and grooming

The art of grooming is divided into two main practices – 'quartering' and full grooming.

Quartering is where the horse's four quarters (both sides of the forehand and both sides of the hindquarters) are groomed by throwing up the rugs but not needing to remove them. It is done by giving the horse a quick brush over with the dandy brush to tidy him up and, usually with the body brush, remove bedding from mane and tail before exercise. The feet are also picked out and the head and 'back end' damp-sponged. Quartering acts in a stimulating way as it is normally done briskly and quickly. Depending on whether or not the horse is actually clipped and rugged up, the body brush and metal curry comb will be used or, on an unclipped horse, the dandy brush.

Full grooming incorporating body brushing is best carried out after exercise or work when the horse has been dried off. The skin will still be warm and supple and easier to clean. The horse will have had a short rest and some food and be amenable and ready for some attention. Also, a regularly groomed horse is easier to clean than one groomed only occasionally.

Start with the dandy brush and possibly the plastic or rubber curry, unless your horse is fine-skinned, sensitive and clipped. (If he is, use the rubber curry and cactus cloth to remove mud and stains – the object is not to scrub at him but to clean him.) The usual advice is to use the left hand for the left side of the horse and vice versa but if you are not fit you will tire and either do a bad job or give up before you have finished one side, so it is fine to change hands. This stage of the grooming stimulates the skin and removes dead hair and caked-on, superficial dirt. Be aware of your horse's level of sensitivity. Brush briskly in the direction of the hair, or occasionally sideways if the mud and dirt are stubborn, and firmly enough to remove the dirt. Every now and then, run your fingers firmly down the bristles (away from the horse) to flick off the dust and hair.

Next take your body brush in one hand and the metal curry comb in the other. The technique for this step is to stand slightly away from the horse and, with your arm stiff (but not rigid) and your elbow slightly bent, place the brush on the coat and *lean your weight* on to the horse to push the bristles through to the skin, making a long, smooth and fairly heavy stroke in the direction of the hair, backwards and downwards. Lift up and repeat, doing two or three strokes before scraping the bristles (facing downwards) across the ridged teeth of the metal curry comb, then doing another two or three strokes. Six strokes in one place should be enough to both clean and massage the underlying structures. Go all over the horse's body like this, building up a rhythm of about one stroke per second which has the effect of calming, reassuring and satisfying both you and your horse. Always be careful of all bony areas such as the head, legs, ribcage, hip bones and so on.

The main purposes of this type of grooming are:

1. To clean the horse's coat and skin.
2. To stimulate the skin and massage the underlying superficial muscles, and to spread the natural oils down the hairs.
3. To encourage the horse to use his muscles and body to lean his weight into yours, thus using, stimulating and self-massaging his deeper musculature.
4. To enhance the circulation of blood and lymph and the flow of life force or energy round the horse's body.

Even on a coat caked with dried mud, many horses object to hard scrubbing with the dandy brush. Flick the dirt up and away from the coat, as shown here. It is always best to groom out of doors whenever possible so as to avoid polluting the stable airspace with dust and also causing the horse to breathe in that dust

When body brushing, it is more effective and less tiring to lean your weight on to the brush with a stiff and slightly bent elbow than to push the bristles through to the skin using your arm and shoulder muscles. It is easier to use the left arm for the left side and vice versa but by all means change hands if you do get tired, otherwise the job may not be done properly

OPPOSITE: *Hot towelling is a really good way to clean horses when it is too cold to wash them. Only very dirty or greasy horses should be washed regularly, in any case. Wearing heavyweight rubber gloves, dip an old terry towel in very hot, clear water and wring it out hard, then fold it quickly (to keep in the heat) into a pad*

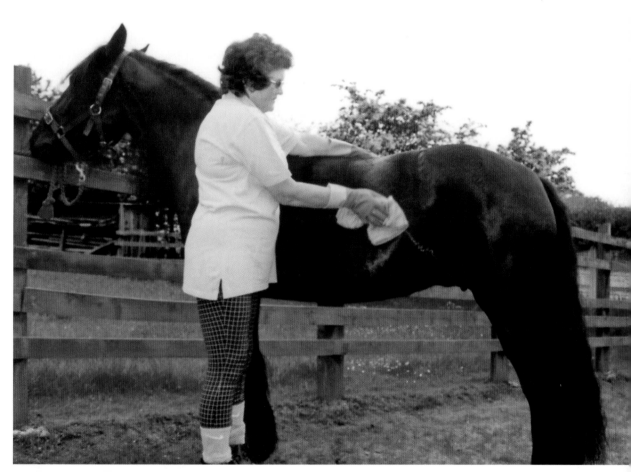

Rub the coat hair firmly *from side to side to raise and remove the dirt and grease. Refold the pad often to expose a clean, hot surface, and regularly rinse the towel and remake your pad as you go*

It takes an inexperienced groom and horse a little while to get used to this technique and its objectives but, once mastered, it results in a horse who is both relaxed and uplifted and a groom who is gradually getting stronger and fitter and has the satisfaction of a job well done. Horses definitely appreciate it and clearly look and feel better for it.

WISPING

Wisping or 'banging' is the final part of the full strapping procedure and is used for skin and coat lubrication and stimulation, and for muscle function, maintenance and development. It has, for generations, been the traditional way of massaging working horses but is seldom seen now other than in the best racing yards, mainly for reasons of time and consequent wages. It involves using a firm pad of twisted and interwoven hay, haylage or soft straw such as oat straw, slapping it carefully but firmly down on the horse's muscular areas and drawing it down as with the body brush. It is, in fact, a combination of the massage techniques *tapotement* and *effleurage* (see Massage under Therapies section). This not only achieves a deep gloss by distributing natural oils throughout the coat and also flattening it but also massages the muscles by squashing and releasing the blood vessels, enhancing the circulation, and causing the muscles to work, as explained below. Again, it is done in a rhythmic, one-a-second routine.

The muscular areas of the horse normally wisped

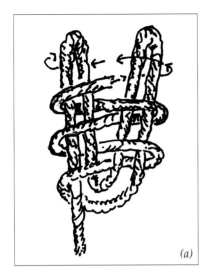

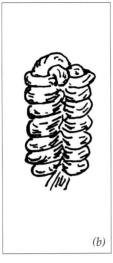

(a) *(b)*

Stages in making a wisp.

(a) Twist a long rope of hay, haylage or soft straw up to about your own height, holding the beginning end under your foot as you twist to give tension. Form the end into two loops slightly longer than your hand and, keeping the beginning under your foot, twist them tightly under the remaining rope as shown in diagram (a)

(b) Tuck the end into the last twist at the top of the wisp to secure it. The finished wisp should be tight, hard and slightly longer than your hand. Jump on it to compact it, and damp it before each use. Depending on how clean or dirty the horse is, a wisp should last for about three or four sessions before you need to make another one. Once you get used to it, this only takes about five minutes. Wisps are far more effective than massage pads

I find that the consensus of opinion (and it's certainly mine) is that it is far better to spend time grooming and wisping (strapping) your horse than to spend the same length of time shampooing and drying him, because the end results are beyond compare.

I realise that it is the fashion today to make life as easy as possible by removing hard work (which also lessens physical fitness) such as correct body brushing and wisping, instead taking the easy way out by washing the horse. Not everything new and up-to-date is good or better than the older ways and I encourage readers to give these techniques a try and not just flick these pages over.

You will find an accompanying illustrated instruction panel for how to make and use a traditional wisp. Today, you can buy massage pads made of leather or chamois with a hand loop which are better than not 'banging' at all, but a hay (or haylage) wisp is by far the best for stimulation of the skin and sliding down the coat; it's also cheap, of course. Leather and chamois pads tend not to slide smoothly down the hair but to pull the skin, which many horses find uncomfortable.

How to do it

The first point to note is that you must completely avoid all bony and sensitive areas of your horse because the wisp is brought down with moderate force on to the body and bruising and injury may arise if you wisp non-muscular areas. The idea is to treat the muscles.

The accompanying drawing shows the areas to wisp. Traditionally, the saddle area on top of the back is not wisped but I was taught as a child by my ex-cavalry riding teacher to wisp this area. The area which bears the saddle (on *top* of the back on *either side* of the spine) consists of thick pads of muscle between the vertical spines or processes of the vertebrae and their transverse (sideways) processes. This area undergoes considerable stress and maybe even injury during riding. The muscles have to work (contract and relax) during movement yet are also subject to considerable compression during this process from the weight of saddle and rider. Sensibly and carefully done, wisping will encourage blood flow to the area and help these compressed muscles to regain their circulation and tone.

43

OPPOSITE: Bring the wisp down with a firm but not hard slap on to a muscle-mass area, the idea being that the horse comes to anticipate the slap and flinches (works) the muscles to brace against it.

Pressing firmly, draw the wisp down the coat in a long stroke which helps to flatten the hair and distribute natural oils through the coat

Take your damped wisp in one hand (your working hand) and stand as for body brushing, slightly away from the horse and with your arm stiff and elbow slightly bent. I know someone who does this job double handed with two wisps or with a wisp in one hand and a stable rubber or cloth in the other.

Slap the flat of the wisp down with your bodyweight on to your chosen area, lean on it and draw it with the lie of the hair, as when body brushing. (The only differences are that in body brushing you do not slap the brush down but place it, and you do not clean the wisp with the metal curry comb!) Lift up and repeat, in rhythm, doing about three to six 'bangs' in one place, then moving on, keeping in rhythm which has a soporific effect on the horse and a 'grounding' effect on the wisper.

The idea of this action is that not only are the muscles and their blood vessels alternately compressed and expanded by the application and release of pressure but also the horse will come to anticipate each slap or bang and will flinch his muscles in anticipation of it and also rhythmically lean into the wisper. This all promotes increased circulation and muscle use. The traditional practice is to take about fifteen minutes on each 'limb' or quarter of the horse (two sides of the front half and two sides of the back half) but almost any time spent on this is better than nothing. Start with five minutes per limb and build up as you get stronger. Turn the wisp when you change sides.

With a horse unused to wisping, initially use light slaps and only one or two in each spot. He will become more used to it with each session until he will let you do a 'proper job' on him. I have always found that horses enjoy being wisped properly.

The normal time for wisping is after body brushing which, in turn, comes after exercise or work. Wisping is meant to promote blood flow to help the muscles get rid of toxins which may have accumulated after work and to bring oxygen and nutrients to the muscles to help them recover. If your horse is undergoing significant work and/or going through a fitness programme, try to wisp every day after grooming. A full strapping by an experienced and competent person should take no more than an hour.

Wisping is also excellent for when you cannot take your horse out due to injury, a lost shoe or some other reason. Obviously, avoid any injured areas. Box-rested horses come through the experience fairly well muscled and physically healthier, in my view, than if they had not been wisped or massaged.

The advantage of wisping over hand massage is that it is comparatively easy, there are no special moves to learn and it equates to both effleurage and tapotement (see section on massage) which are the two simplest techniques for owner-application.

HAND RUBBING

This is a way of cleaning and stimulating the coat and skin and relaxing the horse. It also stimulates the blood, lymph and energy flow through the skin, helps to remove a casting coat and general dead hairs when done with damp hands, dries off a horse when done with dry ones, helps to eliminate toxins from muscles, loosens up tissues and increases the bond between horse and owner. It also puts a terrific gloss on the coat. It was a traditional practice, like the two foregoing ones, until a very few decades ago and is easy, effective and enjoyable for both owner and horse.

Do it with bare hands and forearms (you'll soon warm up in winter) and wipe them on a damp cloth or rinse them as they accumulate grease from the coat during the process. Understandably, it's more pleasant for you to hand-rub a clean horse rather than a dirty one.

On muscular areas, you slap your hands down smartly but not hard on to the coat, and draw them down with firm pressure in the direction of the hair growth. On more sensitive areas such as the throat, ribcage and loins, do not slap your hands on but place them, and firmly but gently stroke in the direction of the hair. Using your forearms as well increases the area treated.

Hand rubbing the legs is a good way to disperse the fluid in filled legs or to help to prevent them in horses on box rest, also to comfort them after work. The lower legs can be gently rubbed and stimulated with palms and fingers, including the backs of the pasterns and heels to

Hand rubbing, demonstrated here by Janet and Lucy, can be done as a relaxation technique, as a stimulating technique or to help dry off a damp coat. Use your flat hands, spread your fingers and rub in the direction of the hair. Forearms can also be used

promote circulation to this vulnerable area. Do the legs carefully *upwards* against the lie of the hair so that you are massaging up towards the heart. Finish off the lower legs by 'rolling' upwards with the heels of your hands to encourage the flow of fluid upwards. Place the heels of both hands on each side of the legs and press in a rolling movement from little finger to thumb, all the way up the lower legs from fetlock to knee or hock. A very gentle version of this upward rolling movement is beneficial in cases of injured tendons and ligaments to help disperse swelling. When rubbing the upper legs where there are muscles (unlike in the lower legs), try using the insides of your forearms and rub upwards towards elbow or stifle.

'Stripping' the ears is another old practice which can be done any time the horse needs relaxing or comforting. Simply place the hands gently around the backs of the ears and pull them towards the tips. Head-shy horses often overcome their fear or anger when used to stripping and most horses eventually drop their heads, close their eyes and enjoy the process.

47

LEADING IN HAND

Few people seem to realise that leading in hand, when done 'with intent' and thoughtfully is an excellent way of maintaining well-being and, of course, of gently exercising a horse coming off box rest or unable to be ridden or turned out for some reason. Many owners will lunge and a few will long rein in these circumstances, but leading in hand can be just as beneficial in its own way. It can be done at walk and trot, as required, and so helps to keep the owner fit, too.

Most owners of livery horses have to put up with restrictive policies regarding grazing and often also the use of the yard's manège or other riding areas. Many yards do not permit loose schooling or, increasingly, even lungeing in their manèges. More and more are, though, installing mechanical horse-walkers and some charge their clients to use them. They may be all very well for yards where, due to economics, a large number of horses has to be exercised in a limited time. Horses do take to walkers and even enjoy their time in them if they are with other horses and their use is not overdone. Half an hour twice a day is enough for any horse. Horse walkers are not a substitute for hand-leading or turnout, but they are better than nothing.

The advantages for the one- or two-horse owner of leading out in hand are several.

- The horse does get to exercise and get his circulation up a little which may otherwise not be possible for reasons given above.
- He can exercise without weight-bearing which may be crucial in cases of back injury where muscle rehabilitation is needed, and in cases of recovering from lameness.
- He gets a change of scenery and to see what is going on around the yard or neighbourhood.
- He gets 'a change of air', although it is hoped his box is well-ventilated anyway.
- He gets a chance to pick at grass and other things on his outings.
- Finally, leading out in hand when, as stated above, it is done thoughtfully and with intent as opposed to being regarded as a chore, is a wonderful way of enhancing the friendship between you and your horse.

The right gear

Dress yourself and your horse according to the weather, your comfort and general safety. If leading out on public tracks or roads, put a high-visibility sheet or rug on him, according to the temperature, and wear a similar tabard and gloves yourself. It would be sensible to wear a hard hat. If you can lead on private routes, rug the horse up sufficiently to keep him warm, as you won't be doing fast work, or not at all in summer. Have a rug which permits free shoulder and foreleg movement, with shaping and darts, but which does not fall down on to the shoulders. The hips and hindlegs must also be able to move freely and not be restricted by over-tight leg straps. A badly fitting rug is quite enough to inhibit a led horse from using himself freely so, in the case of leading for exercise or rehabilitation, this will hamper the process. When you pause for grass, undo the breast strap so that he can graze in comfort and take the chance to bring the rug forward as it will have slipped back a little.

I always prefer to lead horses out in a strong headcollar and nose chain (see illustrations on pages 160 and 162). I find that I have more control with a nose chain than with a bridle and bit as few horses will resist the chain whereas many are used to resisting a snaffle! Also, if one of the reasons you are leading out in hand is for the horse to graze, it will be much more comfortable for him to do this without a bit in his mouth. Some insurance companies now insist on leading in a bridle, though.

Leading in hand, walking or running, is a much under-estimated practice for horse and owner. It has many benefits, gets the handler fit and is an enjoyable way of spending time with your horse. It gives him a change of scene (like taking your dog for a walk) and you can carry out useful physical exercises and techniques. It is safer and more comfortable to use a long lead rope, about half the length of a standard lungeing rein. Many people would also wish to wear a hard hat and gloves. Strong shoes or boots are also advisable

It is also safer to use a half-length lunge rein or double-length leadrope for leading, roughly 12ft or 3.5m long. You can buy these from specialist suppliers, have one made up or simply cut an old lungeing rein in half and oversew the cut end with button thread. (There is no point in putting a hand-loop on it because it is highly dangerous to put your hand and certainly your wrist through a loop when leading an animal as strong as a horse.)

You may also wish to protect the horse's legs with boots, including over-reach boots in front. Your own feet should be in strong boots with reinforced toecaps, not trainers or any kind of plastic or rubber footwear. Toecaps are best made of hardened leather or synthetic material and not metal, which will not spring back should the horse tread on your foot and could make any injury worse.

Amazingly, here in the UK we still often see people leading horses and ponies on public roads on the left but from the left side of the horse. There is this ridiculous tradition, still rampant in some quarters of the horse world, that you should always lead a horse from the left. In fact, for safety and usefulness horses should lead easily and willingly from both sides. Certainly, leading a horse from the left hand side on a public road goes against all common sense road safety and against the Highway Code. Whatever country you live in, always place yourself between the horse and the traffic. Some hair-brained (and air-brained) drivers will not think twice about buzzing a horse but will usually be more careful with a human. Of course, it's always better to lead out away from traffic whenever you possibly can.

As well as wearing high-visibility clothing, I find it a big advantage to lead out with my Tellington white wand (see the section on TTouch). If you don't have one you can paint any old schooling whip white and even tie some fluorescent tape or ribbon on the end. The wand or whip can be held in your hand nearest the traffic as a signal to it to please keep clear, as it is easily visible. (It's a great piece of gear for hacking out with, too.) The whip can also be used behind your back to help control the horse's quarters and to hold out in front of you to help control the forehand and slow down an over-eager horse.

Train your horse to lower his head on command by drawing his attention to something on the ground and saying 'head down'. This is invaluable for getting him to walk with his head down (on the ground or under saddle). Despite being distracted, young Lusitano stallion, Sabio, follows Sheila's lead and body posture and lowers his head

Leading uphill is a good way to get the head down and really stretch the topline muscles as well as encouraging the horse to use the hindquarters strongly

The major points to carry out when leading the horse are to give him free movement of his head and neck, whenever possible, and to encourage him to walk with his head low and swinging, ideally with the poll no higher than the withers. Teaching horses the command 'head down' is useful for all sorts of situations such as calming them down (it works like magic for this), stretching in between spells of ridden schooling and muscular work and for doing things to the head such as bridling or grooming. Out leading, regularly say 'head down' and point to the ground with your whip some distance in front of his head. Lean down a little yourself when you do this and it is surprising how horses pick up on it.

The point about leading out with the head low and freely swinging is to rehabilitate the hard-working and maybe injured back muscles. It really encourages the muscles along the whole of the top line to stretch and move and permit blood, lymph and energy to move readily through them, which is exactly why you are doing this. It also helps keep a horse calm, as mentioned. An excited horse with you on your own two feet is not an appealing prospect,

51

Leading downhill brings the hindquarters under and, again, stretches the topline, especially if one can snatch a snack on the way

especially in public, and making 'head down' a habit can really help, as can automatic and instant obedience to the word 'stand' in any situation.

The type of going underfoot may be an issue. Horses with joint or foot problems, whether injury or disease, should certainly only walk, not trot, on hard going. On the other hand, those with muscle, tendon and ligament problems will not be helped by being made to go in soft ground such as mud, soft sand or a manège with a too-deep surface such as many have today, as it takes an effort to get the foot out of the ground to take the next step and this stresses the soft tissues. Take advice on this point if you are leading out for rehabilitation of any kind.

I find it enjoyable and relaxing to find spots on your route where you can stop, graze, let the horse look around, give him a mint or two which you have brought specially, talk to him, stroke him and generally enjoy some relaxing free time together. People often do this with their dogs but never seem to think about doing it with their horses. When your horse is grazing it is a good opportunity to perform a little one-handed massage, say of his back area, or get him used to ear-stripping whilst he is distracted by the grass. You don't want to irritate him, though, as these walks out are meant to be both beneficial and enjoyable.

To increase flexibility, Kay asks Maddie to flex around a hand placed on her side as she walks along. The idea is to encourage a whole-body flexion, not just a bend in the head and neck. Leading along the fenceline or having an assistant on the outside can help in the early stages. Be sure to do this work to both sides, but slightly more to the side opposite *to that to which the horse flexes most easily*

LUNGEING

Lungeing is one of those activities which are often taken for granted, something which may be done because we haven't time to ride or can't be bothered, or to take the itch out of a horse's heels before we get on and get out. It is something, however, which is often done not only badly but potentially injuriously, the two major faults in its practice being that:

1. Horses are allowed, or encouraged, to go round and round far too fast.
2. Horses are made to go round on circles which are far too small.

These poor techniques put all the wrong stresses on the horse's body, potentially damaging joints, straining tendons and ligaments, stressing muscles and building up all the wrong ones because the horse usually banks on his circles and looks to the outside, both done in order to keep his balance. The horse is fighting the technique instead of allowing it to help him.

Lungeing can certainly be beneficial to horses, both physically as a way of restoring damaged muscles and other tissues to health and re-educating the way of going of a horse who has developed poor action due to injury, and also mentally as a training medium. It is a standard way in many schools of equestrian thought of getting a horse or pony to understand and obey the trainer's vocal requests, of getting him to accept a saddle and also a rider in his early stages of being backed and ridden.

Even lungeing, however, is not the start of it and needs preliminary work if it is to be successful and beneficial and a logical progression of the horse's education. It is quite possible to start handling and lungeing an unhandled, grown-up young horse but it can be quite hair-raising and is not a job for a novice.

Before you start

Ideally, horses should start to be trained or accustomed to the human society into which they have been born from their earliest days. Most good breeders believe that the mare and foal should be left more or less alone, apart from essential services, for their first twenty-four hours together to give them time to get to know each other and bond. After that, though, correct handling should start for the benefit of all. The subject of handling foals and other youngsters is dealt with fully in my book *Modern Horse Breeding*, Swan Hill Press, ISBN 1-84037-032-7.

Whether you are starting with a foal or an older animal, therefore, for the purposes of beginning to lunge him or her it is assumed that the horse is well accustomed to being handled and is *obedient to the voice*. This is a massive help. He should obey 'stand' most importantly so that you can more easily gain control should any situation get out of hand (which is easy with young horses). He should also obey 'walk on', 'over', 'back', 'good boy', and 'no'. An 'umbrella' sort of command such as a long drawn out 'eeeeasy' should be understood as a command to calm down. He should also answer to his name, giving you instant attention.

Another extremely useful command, mentioned earlier, is 'head down' because most rehabilitation and training work involves the horse needing to drop his head to (a) keep calm and (b) allow the muscles of the neck, back and hindquarters to stretch in a bow-shape which will also encourage the hind legs and quarters to tilt under and the belly muscles to come up in support. This is exactly the shape you need to encourage to give the horse a safe posture in which to carry weight or draw a vehicle and, of course, to use his back and topline. 'Head down' can be taught by simply squatting down on the ground or just bending down a couple of feet in front of the horse and pointing to the ground, saying 'head down'. Most horses will look where you are pointing out of curiosity with a little encouragement: the instant he drops his head say 'good boy' and fuss him. He will soon get the idea and the command can be used very usefully from the saddle and on the ground, or when driving.

Whether on the ground or under saddle, I do not use the word 'whoa' to slow down generally. I use 'easy' to calm down at all times including slowing, and I use 'stand' to stop. To go from one gait to another I use the word for the gait I want the horse to adopt, therefore if I am cantering and I want to trot I say 'trot'; if I am walking and I want to stop I say 'stand', if the horse is really messing about I say 'stand' and if I want to canter (whether I am galloping or walking) I say 'can-ter' (or 'walk on' if I am being run off with!).

The horse should be accustomed to being led in hand *equally from both sides* and, during this process, should be accustomed to a command of your choice to tell him to trot, calmly and in a controlled way.

The young horse should also be accustomed to wearing a foal slip and then a headcollar, probably a rug and also protective boots for his legs. If he is used to being handled and groomed, these should not present a problem when they are introduced. Before lungeing, it can be a help if he is used to a roller or saddle and to accepting a bit in his mouth but these are not essential as they can be introduced as the lungeing lessons proceed.

Starting off

There are various ways to train a horse on the lunge. Many trainers have a helper at first but if the horse is experienced at being led in hand even this is not essential.

The horse needs to wear a well-fitting, *sturdy* and probably leather lungeing cavesson, not the type often sold these days which is too flimsy and soft and which pulls round on the horse's head and face with the weight of the rein, rubbing the horse's outside eye and creating an uncomfortable, lopsided pressure on his nose. The cavesson needs a strong, metal ring on the front of a rigid, well-padded noseband to which to attach the lunge rein. There are also usually rings at each side for attaching side-reins, if required.

Your lungeing rein can be of canvas webbing (traditional) or a modern synthetic textile and will be about 20 to 30ft or 6 to 9m in length. It needs a strong clip or buckle at one end to attach to the ring and may have a hand loop at the other which is redundant because it is extremely dangerous to put your hand and wrist through this; even a little pony is quite capable of dragging you and seriously injuring your arm if you cannot get it out of the loop fast enough. Also, although the full length of the rein can and should be used with advantage, it is best to keep a metre or so in reserve to give you a bit of leeway.

In the earliest stages, I am not a believer in kitting the horse out with a roller, saddle, bridle and bit, and certainly not with side-reins unless you have a horse who is very hard to handle when, correctly adjusted, they can give control and discourage dangerous behaviour. If you have a horse like this, seek expert advice.

Use a well-fitting lungeing cavesson, protective leg boots, over-reach boots and your lungeing rein to start with.

A lungeing whip is a big help in directing the horse *if* you are practised enough to use it effectively and safely. It should be light and stiff and have a lash and thong. The rod part of the whip will be something over 4ft or 1.2m long and the lash should be about 4 ½ yards or 4m long or a little more. The rod part of modern whips will be of a good, lightweight and stiff

Opposite: Rose models a well-fitting lungeing cavesson. This is one of the nylon web kind readily available today. They are not so stable on the head as a well-made and fitted but more expensive leather cavesson with a padded noseband

How to fit a cavesson and bridle together. The cavesson goes on top of the bridle, but the bridle cheekpieces are brought outside the cavesson noseband to prevent interference with the bit. The bridle noseband is removed and the reins can be secured out of the way by the cavesson and/or bridle throatlatch or removed altogether

material but the thong part may be of lightweight synthetic material which kinks and does not run out well. If you can get, or have made, a whip with a synthetic rod and leather thong, this would be ideal.

You need to practise using the whip – handling it so that you can put it anywhere you want with ease, and running out the lash so that you can flick a tin can off a log with accuracy. The purpose of the whip is to direct and guide the horse and sometimes you need to *touch* (never hurt) him with the lash on the end of the thong to move him on or out on to the circle.

Early sessions

You don't need the whip just yet. With your handler standing by, stand on one side of the horse and have your excess lunge rein coiled in your same hand, so if you are on the horse's right the rein is coiled in your right hand and vice versa. Hold the rein an easy distance from the ring with your other hand and ask the horse to 'walk on'. Walk quite calmly, looking ahead and not at the horse which can inhibit him, and very gradually feed out a little rein and walk further away from him. Eventually, the horse may feel that he is too far away from you and may start wandering towards you: now ask your helper to come to the other side of the horse and attach a leadrope to that side ring on the cavesson so that he or she can calmly but positively guide the horse out on to a circle (leaving the vocal aids to you).

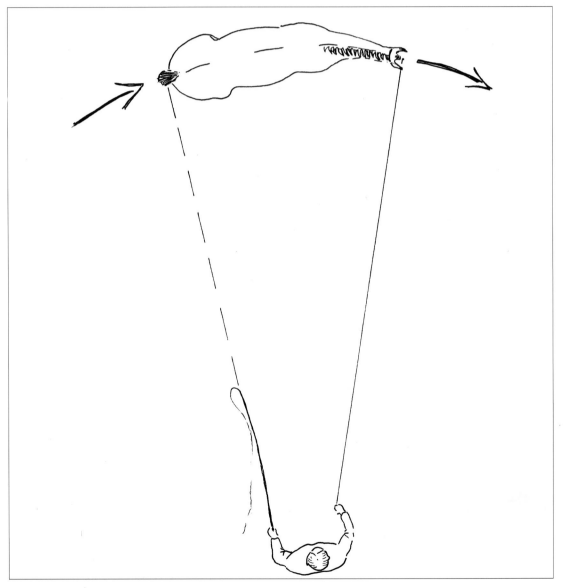

Body language is a great help when lungeing. The trainer should form the apex of a triangle made by the horse, the lungeing rein and whip, and the trainer, as shown. By moving slightly more towards the horse's hips or his head, the trainer can, respectively, urge the horse on or slow or stop him

Do a couple of circles, not too large at first, in one direction then a couple in the other, eventually building up to full-size circles with a radius almost the length of the lunge rein. When the horse gets the idea, take up your whip, keep the handler who should by now be able to maintain a quite loose lead rope, and tuck the whip, lash behind you, under your arm which is not holding the rein.

Where you stand is crucial and amounts to 'body language' which the horse will understand. If you stand facing his hip and point the whip behind him or at his hocks it encourages the horse to go on; if you stand level with his shoulder and point the whip there it has a slowing effect. Pointing the whip in front of him, and holding it up, coupled with the word 'stand', which he ought to know, should stop him: if it doesn't, your helper should assist and help to stop the horse.

Allowing the horse a few minutes of high jinks is the subject of disagreement. With a horse being rehabilitated you would not want to allow this for fear of further injury but when lungeing as a means of getting the itch out of a horse's heels he will normally settle quicker into his work after a few minutes of play provided he is warmed up first to help avoid injury

Once you can stand in the centre of the circle he is describing and use your whip, pointing at his centre, to keep him out, and he does this calmly in walk to both reins, try a few steps of trot with the helper still guiding. Proceed this way until the horse regards lungeing as a calm, non-hassle procedure in which he listens to his trainer in the centre. At this point, dispense with the helper. The horse should not associate lungeing with whizzing round and round incessantly, too fast which is damaging, and leaning in and probably flexing out to keep his balance, on too-small circles, all of which can be very injurious to his muscles, tendons, ligaments and joints.

From a bodywork viewpoint, it pays to get an expert assessment of your horse's physical condition. Your attending veterinary surgeon or other therapist should be able to give you information about which muscles need building up, using and stretching, if you cannot see it yourself (and it takes education and experience), and maybe give you a programme to follow.

From a physical maintenance viewpoint, twenty or thirty minutes two or three times a week in a correct, voluntarily assumed outline (that is without tight side-reins or unforgiving 'gadgets' which simply force the position) is ample to keep the horse using himself freely without weight. Remember to keep the circles large and encourage the horse to go with his head down, pushing from behind, and flexing slightly inwards so that he is looking where he is going along the circumference of the circle. Do not keep exclusively to circles but perform straight lines (running with the horse), ovals and varied circles from medium to large.

A big and common mistake when lungeing is to keep the lunge rein coiled in and cause the horse to go on too small a circle. This is stressful and potentially injurious to his muscles and leg joints. Do not be afraid to let the rein out almost fully, as shown here by Tracey and her Thoroughbred Elementary dressage horse, Cyril The Squirrel

Here, Cyril demonstrates walking on a long lunge rein with his head down, stretching his whole topline long and low. He is wearing protective bandages with padding, and over-reach boots. The saddle here is not needed but many people use the saddle to fit side reins to the girth straps. Tracey prefers the means of attaching the lungeing rein as shown which many feel gives more control, with the rein clipped to the outside bit ring, brought up over the poll, down through the inside bit ring and to the trainer's hand. Only skilled and sensitive trainers should lunge a horse from the bit: others should use a cavesson with the rein clipped to the front ring

Pole work can and should be introduced to teach the horse to use himself properly, and little grids of small cross-pole jumps encourage him to think and move straight and to lift his forelegs and shoulders as well as pushing straight off from behind.

Other equipment such as bridles and bits (many experienced people like to lunge from the bit), saddles, rollers and maybe a chambon for a horse who is having problems getting the 'head down' part, can be added as is thought necessary. There are complete books on lungeing and it is a good plan to study one to get the best out of this technique.

Tellington lungeing

In the Therapies section, there is information on a technique called TTouch which is part of the

61

TTEAM (Tellington Touch Equine Awareness Method) system. This is part of an entire riding, training and rehabilitation system part of which is the TTeam version of lungeing.

This involves using a half-length lunge rein and the white schooling-length whip called the wand, rather than a conventional lungeing whip. This does attract and keep the horse's attention better than a dark whip. It is used in the same hand as that in which you hold the lunge rein. Some users do find it easier to use the wand in the other hand, however.

The headgear is an ordinary headcollar with a nose chain, either the type detailed in the section on leading in hand or the more usual American method illustrated here.

In this method, the trainer/handler walks much more with the horse, and performs the work in ovals and other shapes, rather than standing in the middle of a circle. I like this method very much. Many owners feel that it is easier and gives more control for those unused to lungeing – horse or human, and the half-length rein is easier to handle than the longer one. Some feel that the fact that you have to move more with the horse is a disadvantage but it does help you to get fitter!

Two particular items of TTeam body equipment can be used when doing groundwork including lungeing, both of which help the horse to go better depending on his temperament. There is the 'body rope' which is draped in a figure-of-eight way around the horse's body and which encourages reluctant or lazy horses to go forward, and the 'body wrap' made from soft, stretchy bandages which is good for more nervous horses who either rush or do not relax.

ABOVE AND OPPOSITE: *Pauline and Rose try Tellington lungeing (covered later) for the first time. It is carried out with a special Tellington lead or with a half-length lungeing rein, and with the Tellington white wand held, as a guide, in the same hand. The trainer walks more with the horse and it is a very versatile system*

Jumping. Hussein showing good lift of the forehand and good impulsion from the hind legs. This is a suitable jump for a young horse to gain experience without the disturbance of a rider

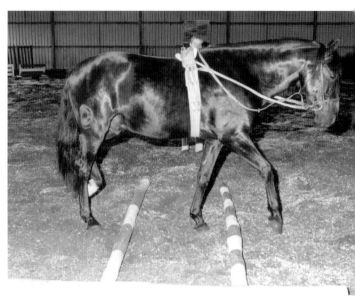

Nero walking over poles. The horse is using his neck, back and right fore and left hind, with the right fore absolutely central followed by the left hind. This will cause the horse to 'give' with his loin muscles. Notice the horse's concentration

Nero working on the lunge preparatory to liberty work. The handler holds two short whips: in the left hand the whip indicates to the horse to stop, whilst the right-hand whip is inactive but ready to ask for 'walk on' as the left whip is lowered. The horse is watching the handler attentively

LONG-REINING

Ask most horse owners if they ever long-rein their horses and they will say 'no' but ask them if they lunge them and the answer varies from 'yes' to 'sometimes'. I always find this surprising because long-reining gives much more control than lungeing if you're expecting problems, produces a more beneficial movement from the horse than lungeing and can actually take a horse from breaking in or starting to High School work without his ever being sat on.

Once your horse lunges well and is obedient to the voice, you can progress to long-reining with advantage. Although you have two reins to cope with, you also have more freedom in how and where you ask your horse to move, changing rein is easier and you can switch smoothly from long-reining, where you walk more or less behind the horse most of the time, to what can be termed two-rein lungeing where you stand mainly in the middle of a circle.

Long-reining is also good for exercising a horse under controlled conditions out and about around his neighbourhood, particularly if you have a helper accompanying you. The technique is used to teach the horse hand aids in conjuction with using the voice (the horse should already be obedient to vocal commands) without the extra mental and physical burden of carrying a rider or having to think about leg aids, although the reins along the sides of his body act as direction. The technique also supples the horse and can encourage impulsion and a correct way of going ('both ends down and the middle up') and offers the horse much more variety in his work than basic lungeing. It is an excellent technique for re-educating injured or improperly used muscles, gaits and way of going and it also provides your horse – and you – with entertainment and education.

I find that horses like long-reining whereas many do not particularly like being lunged. I had an old Thoroughbred mare who had been broken in by means of long-reining in a conventional English flat-racing yard as a yearling in the 1970s. I was fairly sure that she had not been long-reined for many years before I bought her at the age of twenty-three and when the Head Lad at her livery yard (who is from a traditional racing background and served his apprenticeship with one of Britain's best old horseman-type racehorse trainers) suggested that he long-rein her out for me on the days I could not visit, I was very interested to see what she would do.

I made sure I was there the first time out of curiosity. I trusted the Head Lad implicitly as did my mare and she inspected his gear with interest as he tacked her up. As he finished, she was facing away from the door looking out of her back window. As soon as he picked up the reins (without saying a word) she turned, came into outline and marched straight out of the box door towards the gateway. She clearly knew what was going on. Her face was interested and knowing and stayed that way all the way round the short route we had chosen. He long-reined her out for the rest of her life and they both loved it. We used to joke that he could long rein her down the main road through the village with *The Daily Mail* in one hand and a cigarette in the other.

(This is also an interesting example about the length and strength of horses' memories. She

OPPOSITE: *Throughout my adult riding life, I have been inspired by the techniques and abilities of Miss Sylvia Stanier, LVO, one of the most skilled exponents in the world of lungeing and long-reining, as well as classical riding to the highest level. She has allowed the use of these and other photographs (by Peter Sweet) for this book and has written the captions herself. The horses shown in this section are the Arabian stallion Hussein and the Lusitano stallion Nero, both working on the lunge*

hadn't forgotten a thing and loved leading the way but waiting for directions – even though some behavioural scientists claim that long-reining is a form of domination because the horse is being 'herded' from behind as if by a stallion moving his band.)

Equipment

Long reins the length of lungeing reins (20 to 30ft or 6 to 9m) are fine to use although traditional long reins as used to train driving horses are normally longer at up to 46ft or 14m. The more rein you have the more room you can give your horse but the more excess rein you then have to cope with in each hand. (The Spanish Riding School method of long-reining uses roughly half-length reins and the trainer walks very closely behind the horse.) The normal webbing reins can be rather heavy to handle and if you can get, or have made, some rounded, braided rope reins, synthetic or otherwise, they should be lighter and less bulky, especially if you have small hands. These also run more easily through the D-rings or rein terrets on a roller or the stirrups if using a saddle.

Selle Français gelding, Rouche, tacked up simply for long-reining. He wears a bridle without reins, a saddle and has the long reins running from the bit, through the stirrups to the trainer's hands. The stirrup irons are tied together under his girth area for safety and stability. Here a length of binder twine is used effectively but some prefer to use a stirrup leather of just the right length so that there is no flapping end to distract the horse. As with lungeing, only skilled trainers should long rein direct from the bit, otherwise a lungeing cavesson should be used

You will also need either a proper driving roller with rein terrets for the Danish method or a comfortable, well-fitting driving or breaking roller with D-rings, or a saddle and stirrups, for the English method. (See below for descriptions of the methods.)

The driving roller has rein terrets which are used according to the horse's level of training, the lower ones being used for green horses to encourage them to lower and round and the higher ones for horses coming into collection.

The English method can be carried out without a roller of any kind, or a saddle, but either will give more support to and control of the reins. A breaking or driving roller will have D-rings, and the saddle is used with stirrups through which the long reins pass. As most people will have a saddle, there is no need to buy a roller.

The stirrups should be fastened together beneath the horse's belly, usually with a stirrup leather, to stop them swinging around.

Methods

There are various types of long-reining (and many people make up their own methods after some experience) but the main one I'll consider here is the traditional English method but with mention of the excellent Danish method used for many years by Miss Sylvia Stanier LVO (taught to her by Mr Einar Schmit Jensen) and of which she has given high-profile demonstrations with High School horses. Again, both techniques are well covered in more detailed books.

The English method of long-reining involves fastening each long rein to the ring of a snaffle bit or to the rings on a conventional lungeing cavesson. In the latter case it would help greatly to have two extra rings set on the noseband towards the back at about seven o'clock and five o'clock as this will give a more direct feel on the noseband. The outside rein passes down the horse's side, through the stirrup if a saddle is being used, and comes round behind the gaskins to the trainer's hand. The inside rein can pass directly to the trainer's hand or through the stirrup. The trainer can be behind the horse, can move to either side or stand more in the centre of a circle, in which cases the outside rein helps to control the hindquarters.

Some horses, particularly those not used to such things as fillet strings or leg straps, can kick up a real fuss when they first feel the rein round their thighs; horses completely unused to this procedure should be schooled first of all by an experienced trainer. To begin with, the horse should be stood still and held by a competent helper whilst the trainer moves around him, letting him feel the long reins on his sides and round his thighs. With the helper leading him, or maybe even one on each side if you are expecting difficulties, and the trainer behind him, he should then be asked to move off at a walk and very gradually accustomed to the feel of the reins on straight lines and turns, progressing from there.

The Danish method has ultimately both reins passing through the selected terrets on the roller, once the horse is used to them, and passing from them directly to the trainer's hands. Initially, one rein can act as a lungeing rein and the outside rein only be passed through a terret. It is important to get the horse initially used to the feel of the reins on his back as, in this method, there is no outside rein around the quarters and the trainer changes direction by passing behind the horse and lifting the reins up over the horse's back as he performs an S-bend, being led through his changes initially by the helper.

Dawn long-reins Rouche uphill, asking him to stretch forwards and down. This encourages strong use of the hindquarters and legs and stretches the top line muscles whilst encouraging the horse to lift his belly. Most horses do this naturally but some trainers actually prevent it by holding the hands too high and the reins too tightly. Dawn is not using a whip

---

Going downhill brings the hind end underneath and helps to develop balance. In the system of long-reining Dawn uses, the right rein has been released here to encourage the horse to turn left

Rose and Pauline practise long-reining down the drive. Pauline is using a Tellington wand rather than a longer whip

When long-reining, the handler/trainer walks or runs behind the horse or, preferably, slightly behind the horse's inside hip, holding one rein in each hand and also often a buggy whip, stiff and of lightweight synthetic material. A buggy whip is almost the length of a lungeing whip but has no thong. The long reins may also be held in one hand, separated by the fingers – usually one rein between the little and ring fingers and one between the middle and index fingers – and the whip held in the free hand although most trainers use both hands. The whip, as with the lungeing whip, is used to indicate impulsion and direction to the horse. At first, it should be held, lash backwards, under one arm till the horse gets used to things, then gradually be accustomed to the sight of it.

The trainer may work a little closer to the horse than in conventional lungeing, but it depends on where you feel happiest. The closer you are the more control you have but perhaps a distance of about 13ft or 4m will feel about right.

How to proceed

After a successful, short lungeing session of, say, ten or fifteen minutes, and with a helper if available, tack up as for long-reining and let the horse stand with your helper, as described, and get him used to the reins touching him. If you start off by walking behind the horse with your helper leading him or at least walking by his head, and just ask for 'walk on', most horses will set off very well and only start to worry, if at all, when they feel the reins. This is why it is so important to accustom the horse to them at halt.

Certainly for your first session, just walk around your schooling area, which should be an indoor school or a properly fenced outdoor manège. Do not try this, or any new technique or manoeuvre, in a large, open field in case the horse takes fright and gets free.

It is important to keep your hands light and sensitive and not to adopt a dead, pulling feel on them. You are, in fact, riding on the ground so your outside rein controls the balance and speed whilst the inside one talks to the horse and asks for flexion.

Of course, in long-reining you can easily ask the horse to work on straight lines and walk on with impulsion, gradually taking up an outline. You will find that the work makes you fit, if you are not already, because you can ask for walk, trot and even canter as the horse becomes more advanced and you transfer to working with the reins attached to the bit of a bridle instead of the rings of a lungeing cavesson.

As mentioned, the finer points should be studied in one of the various books on these techniques, but from a bodywork viewpoint, the movements which can be carried out on long reins and which are beneficial to the horse's development and rehabilitation are:

- Again asking the horse to go with 'head down' to remind him of beneficial body posture, plus gentle feels on the inside rein to help attain 'give' and correct flexion in all movements.
- Moving with impulsion in a reasonable outline, as he progresses in all gaits.
- Asking for slight inside flexion on all circles and bends.
- Turns, progressing to S-bends, serpentines, loops, circles and figures-of-eight.
- Changes of rein whilst maintaining good posture.
- Transitions from one gait to another and also within gaits from shortened to lengthened strides and back again, maintaining good outline.
- Halts and immobility – teaches patience and discipline!
- If you progress to working outdoors, hill work, both up and down, is beneficial to the horse

without having to carry a rider.
- Pole work and grids and small fences can be enjoyable and beneficial provided correct way of going is maintained

Check with your therapist, if applicable, which type of work would be best for the horse according to his particular physical problem. If this does not apply, just work as if riding, asking for your various movements and using the reins correctly, never pulling backwards to force the horse into an outline but tactfully 'holding his hand' with the outside rein and 'talking' down the inside one.

As well as benefiting your horse one thing is certain – it will get you fit if you aren't already!

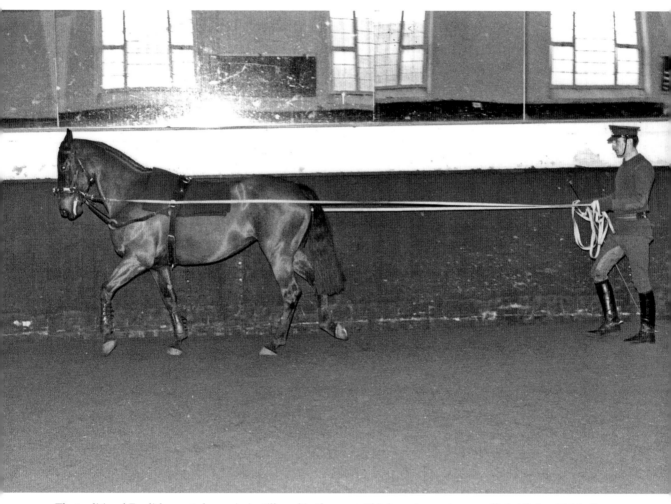

The traditional English way to long rein is still used in the army. This horse is wearing a snaffle bridle to which both the long reins and the side reins are fitted and a lungeing cavesson. A horse may start his session working off the cavesson, the reins later being transferred to the bit rings. The horse also wears a blanket pad and a driving roller with dees, the reins passing through the lower dees as for a novice horse. Many trainers would add a crupper to prevent the roller riding forwards (Photo: Clive Hiles)

71

Miss Stanier with the Andalusian/Spanish stallion Pedro shows the transition from Piaffe to Passage – see the handler's action to push the horse forward without him losing balance. (The front, left foot is as high as the knee, the right hind at hock height ready to push forward.) Correct flexion of pasterns (Photo: Peter Sweet)

The Oldenburg stallion Adel shows shoulder-out (on three tracks, flexion to the wall, handler and reins on the left side of the horse) (Photo: Peter Sweet)

Adel in extended trot, showing extension of left fore forwards and left hind extending backwards, as is the right fore, right hind engaging for propulsion (Photo: Peter Sweet)

Pedro in Spanish Walk or March, weight well onto hindquarters. Unfortunately, the right hind is not shown as walking forwards (Photo: Peter Sweet)

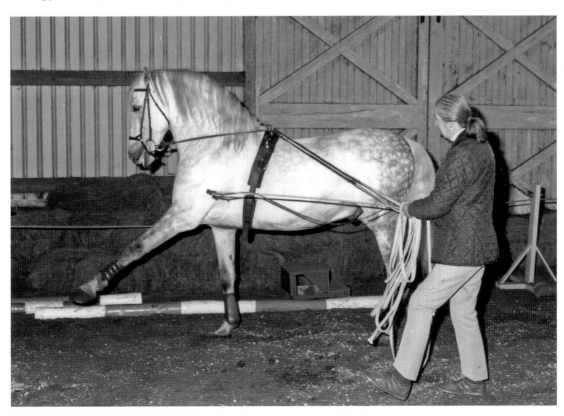

RIDING

It may seem strange to see riding listed as a management technique when it is mainly *because* we ride and work our horses that they have problems. Horses often have problems due to being ridden because (a) they are ridden incorrectly in relation to the natural functioning of their muscles which brings about inappropriate muscle use, and (b) they are asked to perform feats which are beyond them as individuals, possibly due to lack of talent, athletic fitness and muscle strength.

If we ride them in such a way as to not only allow their muscles to function as they were meant to but also strengthen and develop them, horses' problems would surely be reduced.

Just because a horse is ridden at top levels of competition because he has the talent and has the sort of human connections who wish to ride in this milieu, it does not always mean, surprisingly, that he is being ridden correctly or appropriately as far as his physical functioning

The muscular development on this Thoroughbred dressage horse, Cyril The Squirrel, shows the results of correct and regular gymnastic work under saddle following the principles of classical riding

This Thoroughbred mare, Madison (Maddie), is well fed, looked after and ridden but not gymnastically worked, so she does not show the same muscle development. She performs well for her owner.

and maintenance is concerned. It is most noticeable that some world-level horsemen and women seem very frequently to appear on new and different horses whereas others compete at a high level on the same ones for several, even many, years. The obvious conclusion to draw from this phenomenon is that the horses who seem to compete satisfactorily for years in the same hands are ridden well and suitably for them whereas others possibly are not.

A clear example of the success of correct riding techniques is seen at The Spanish Riding School in Vienna. The display horses are Lipizzaner stallions and although most riders, particularly those in specialised competitive fields, do not aspire to the performance of High School airs, the stallions of Vienna often work hard well into their twenties. The movements they perform are extremely physically taxing but because they have been correctly trained and physically developed from their youth they are permanently kept in a condition fit and strong enough to perform these airs for many years with minimal chances of injury.

Of course, there are all sorts of reasons for horses to disappear from the competitive scene such as being sold on to people less suited to them, ageing taking its normal toll, riders giving up, horses having accidents, temperament and personality clashes, illness and so on. Horses may also disappear from the scene because they are simply 'bled dry' – overworked and used rather than paced and cared for. Good, appropriate riding must play a major part in good management even though it is often thought of as a procedure apart from care. Riding and stable management have long been separated in equestrian exams almost as if they are not connected whereas good riding is part of good management.

The horse's basic anatomy and physiology – how he is made and how he works – have been basically discussed in Section 1 of this book. Here, we'll look at how the muscles and other structures should be employed and 'trained' in order to produce a correctly and safely muscled-up horse, and at techniques to achieve this. We'll also look at incorrect techniques and consider some of their results.

What do I mean by 'safe'? I mean a horse who can carry a rider's weight (which will be around a sixth of his own) without undue risk of physical distress, strain and resultant injury to himself. Because horses were not designed or evolved to carry weight, it does undoubtedly burden them when we sit on them. They were not designed to push into a collar or breast harness in order to 'pull' a vehicle behind them, either. Driving horses and ponies develop injuries peculiar to their job in the same way that jumpers, racehorses and dressage horses do.

Good riding helps horses in two main, physical ways:

1. It acts as a damage limitation exercise by at least doing the horse no harm.
2. It strengthens and develops the muscles the horse needs to use to both
   carry our weight and do the work we ask of him.

Bad riding and balance, on the other hand, depending on their nature, hamper and harm the horse in the following ways:

1. By causing him to expend a lot of muscular effort and energy bracing his muscles against the burden on his back.
2. By forcing him constantly to adjust his muscles to enable him to move as normally as he can under this unstable weight, or even to stay on his feet.
3. An intrusive rider who gives commands to the horse which the horse is not physically capable of carrying out over-stresses the horse's physique, because most horses *will* try to carry out these commands.
4. The horse will usually become at least dull and resigned to his lot, 'difficult' or frequently unsound.

The horse can easily end up not only trying to balance himself and his rider and carry out difficult physical feats for which he is not prepared but also physically trying to avoid the discomfort and pain occasioned by these attempts, plus that caused by harsh, inappropriate movements of the rider such as jabs in the mouth or kicks in the ribs which are even more painful if spurs are worn. This is no way to build up and strengthen the muscles the horse actually needs for his job or to maintain a balanced, pain-free body, not to mention a good relationship.

Moving weight

The structures which actually move the horse are his muscles. In general, the skeleton is the framework, the ligaments are the binding and the muscles are the engines which move the rest. You only have to look at any horse to see that he is forehand-heavy, that is he carries most of his weight on his forehand. The head and neck are heavy and this weight can only be passed down through the shoulders to the forelegs which have to carry both it, the weight of the shoulders and of the thorax or chest and its contents, transmitted via the backbone through the soft tissues which bind the forelegs to the ribcage. The hind legs carry the weight of the hindquarters plus the weight of the abdominal contents transmitted to them, again, via the backbone through the hip joints

The legs begin at the shoulders and the hips, not the elbows and stifles. The forelegs have a significant weight-bearing job to do as the knee is rigid when weight is passing over it, but concussion is absorbed mainly in the foot, fetlock, elbow and shoulder joints which flex to lessen the impact and help bear the weight passing over the leg. The hindlegs' main function is propulsive. The horse should push himself along, mainly, from the hindquarters which are the engine for the whole body although horses with back, hindquarter and hind leg injuries often learn to haul themselves along more with the muscles of the forehand and back. This clearly makes for incorrect muscle development when it comes to work.

It is most interesting to study the differing muscle development in horses who have been worked correctly, those who have been worked incorrectly and those who have not been worked at all. The commonest 'sins' in riding appear to be:

- To allow a horse to work 'on the forehand' which results in over-development of the forearm and shoulder muscles.
- To haul the head in and overbend the horse which causes pain and damaged soft tissues.
- To not give the horse enough relaxation and stretch periods during a schooling session which, again, causes pain plus stiffness, tissue damage and a 'muscle bound' horse.

An incorrect way of going can actually cause bone damage due to muscles being torn away at their origins (normally) and insertions, and damaging the bone in the process. If this happens near a joint, the joint's function and future viability can be adversely affected although joints are also badly affected by concussion, torsion (twisting) forces and excessive stress and strain. A common sequel to bone damage is osteoarthritis.

Unfortunately for horses, many of we humans are 'front-end fixated' whereas we ought to be 'back-end fixated'. Many of us look at the head and neck carriage of a working horse and also his foreleg action and may think he looks tremendous but we should be looking at the hindquarters and hindlegs to see if they look equally tremendous and are, most importantly, engaging and *working* to push the horse forward from his engine. Because so many of us concentrate on the head and neck and have heard about such things as 'collection', being 'on the bit' and 'extended' gaits, we trawl tack stores for any gadget which we think will help us to achieve an 'upward, rounded and backward' forehand posture (as it was once described to me by a new client).

The fact that so many people think that a horse should go with his neck up and rounded and his chin tucked in towards, or even touching, his chest is a frightening indictment of the misunderstandings which seem to be present in riding today and, as a shiatsu practitioner as well as a teacher of classical riding, I am sure that horses made to go like this (because they certainly do not move like this voluntarily) experience pain in the poll, jaw, neck, shoulders and back because of the wrong use of what *could* be perfectly helpful training aids, and the lack of understanding of how a riding horse should move.

I have seen horses trained in this way standing in the stable and field who looked, to me, muscle bound and stiff and unable to eat from ground-level in comfort. This is heart-breaking but their owners and riders purposely aim for this because they genuinely think that an over-developed neck and shoulders (due to excessive and incorrect muscle use) looks good.

We have to face the fact that if we are going to sit on our horses and expect them to move in particular ways under us we are going to put them at a disadvantage. We can lessen this and help a horse to progress if we:

- Make sure that our saddle, bridle and bit really fit and suit the horse, otherwise he will not relax but will stiffen against discomfort and his muscle use will be disadvantaged.
- Ride correctly and as well as possible if we are going to minimise their burden.
- Make sure that we keep our horses as sound as possible and do not pass off minor problems.
- Ensure that we do not overburden our horses by under-horsing ourselves – we need a horse up to our weight. It is generally felt that a sound horse can carry a sixth of his own weight reasonably easily.
- Enable the horse to perform well by learning how to work him gymnastically to develop and maintain his muscles and body.
- Make sure that his heart and lungs are kept healthy and fit enough for his job.
- Ensure that his nutrition is suitable for him as an individual and for his work.

All this is quite a tall order and some of the requirements are outside the scope of this book although there are other excellent books which will give you the main knowledge you need. This book covers bodywork and this section covers bodywork under saddle – correct basic riding and schooling for optimal muscular development, strength and maintenance, and a starting point from which to progress.

Tack and its effects

If you watch a horse moving at liberty you are watching him at his most able with no encumbrances – no weight, no saddle, no bit and no tight straps constricting him anywhere. Once we start putting on tack and sitting on him his problems start. The first way of keeping our interference to a minimum is to make sure that every piece of tack we use fits him perfectly and is adjusted *comfortably*. Any discomfort causes anxiety, irritation and resistance in the form of muscular evasion and incorrect use (compensatory movement) and possibly muscle spasm and injury if the situation continues. To enlarge on what was discussed earlier, here are some basic points of tack fit:

- The bridle must not impinge on the ears or eyes.
- The bit must be the correct height, the most usual fault being that it will be too high in the mouth. If it is too high it will cause discomfort, resistance, unhappiness and reduced willingness and performance.
- The noseband must *not* be tight, contrary to current fashion. If the noseband is too tight it may well restrict the horse's breathing which is an important consideration because horses cannot breathe through their mouths. If the jaws are strapped tightly closed this will certainly prevent the horse 'giving' or flexing to the bit when the rider asks him to do so, therefore the rider is very effectively preventing the horse doing what the rider is asking for.

- The saddle must be extremely comfortable and evenly stable on the horse's back and should be fitted, and checked every few months, by a trained, qualified saddle *fitter*.
- It must not be tight and too narrow. Pressure under the tree points and stirrup bars (just behind and below the withers) in particular, from poorly distributed weight and a too-tight fit, cause significant and chronic muscle injury and even loss of use.
- You should be able to see a clear tunnel of daylight all the way down the gullet and be able to fit three fingers' width between the pommel and withers when the horse's heaviest rider is in the saddle.
- You must be able to fit the side of your hand between the front of the saddle and the back edge of the top of the shoulder blade just below the wither, otherwise the shoulder movement and the horse's muscle use will be hampered. Also, if the saddle is put on too far forward, the saddle will probably be tilted up at the pommel so the rider will inevitably slide back towards the cantle and the stirrup leathers will pull his or her feet forwards from the stirrup bars; the rider will be well out of balance with the horse.
- At the back, the panel below the cantle must *not* press down into the back muscles or, certainly, rest on the loins as this will bruise the muscles and favour the horse hollowing instead of raising his back – exactly the opposite to what you want – and prevent free, swinging, forward movement.
- The girth must not be so far forward as to come into contact with the horse's elbow area when he brings his forelegs back. This can cause girth injuries and, again, will certainly inhibit the horse from moving freely and correctly.
- The girth should not need to be so tight that you cannot fit the flat of four fingers fairly easily between it and the horse.

How should the horse go?

When the horse is at liberty and moving as he wishes, provided he is healthy and sound his use of his body is perfect for his needs (although you may notice that few horses go perfectly 'straight' with their hind feet following exactly in the tracks of the fore). When he carries the weight of a rider, however, he has to adapt his way of going to support that weight without using his muscles unnaturally.

All he has to do, in fact, is learn to make more use of a movement which is natural to him every time he raises his forehand – getting up, cantering and galloping, jumping and so on. To do this, he lifts up in front using mainly the superficial and deep muscles of his hindlegs, hindquarters, loins and back. In the context of flat work, ridden or otherwise, this action is supported by the belly muscles working from underneath and also the muscles underneath the lower neck vertebrae.

The use and co-ordination of muscles in the moving horse is very complex, but basically the horse has to go, to adopt a safe, weight-carrying posture, with his spine inclined upwards and his hindquarters 'flexed' or tilted under (by the use of the muscles under the loins and attached to the massive thigh bones) at a joint called the lumbo-sacral joint which is at the point of the croup. This tilting under of the hindquarters and the consequent bringing forward of the hindlegs, which are joined to the pelvis at the hip joints, are what 'engage' the horse's hind end.

The vertebral column has a very slight upward 'bow' to it which is a strong structure for bearing weight – in the horse's case in the form of the heavy abdominal contents which are slung by very strong membranes and connective tissue from underneath the spine and the

OPPOSITE: *No horse will work at his best if he is not comfortable and tack fit and adjustment are crucial to this. A particularly unkind fashion is to have bits too high and nosebands too tight. Cyril is wearing an ordinary eggbutt snaffle bit which is making the correct* one *wrinkle at the corners of the lips so the skin is not pulled tight and uncomfortably. His flash noseband allows for two fingers to be passed comfortably underneath the flash part …*

… BELOW: *and also the cavesson part, and the cavesson section is adjusted low enough to prevent rubbing of the facial bones*

Walking work under saddle for rehabilitation or for warming up (before working in) should involve the horse going with his head down and forward, ideally with the poll below the withers, to stretch the soft tissues along the entire top line, and the rider adopting a light seat. It is a major mistake to expect the horse to work 'in an outline' all the time, from start to finish of a session, as the muscles do not get a chance to stretch, relax, and let the blood and lymph flow freely through them both in preparation for work and to provide oxygen and nutrients. Stretching and relaxation also remove waste products during breaks in a work session, helping to maintain the health of the soft tissues

undersides of the top parts of the ribs. The horse needs to raise the spine a little, exaggerating its natural 'vertebral bow'. The neck also needs to be lifted at its base by the muscles underneath its lower vertebrae which gives the effect of the neck coming up in front of the withers.

The actual carriage of the head and neck depend on the horse's stage of training. The neck should always be pushed up from the base and forwards: novice horses need to develop this posture by going 'long and low' *with the poll about level with the withers and the nose in front of the vertical*, whilst more advanced horses able to go in collection go with the neck carried higher and the front of the face on or slightly in front of the vertical.

The state of collection naturally moves the horse's weight back more on to the hindquarters and it takes time, months at least depending on your starting point, for the muscles to develop the strength and endurance to hold the body in this posture under weight and for longer periods than the free horse would adopt. It is, though, a natural posture for the horse; it just needs developing.

The mistake many riders make, even some of those competing in the higher levels of dressage and show jumping, is to draw the horse's head in from the front, with or without 'gadgets' or incorrectly-used training aids, even to the point where the front of the face is behind the vertical, sometimes well behind it. Some riders appreciate the need for the horse to engage behind and send the energy forwards but combined with a harsh, enforced and overbent head carriage the result is great discomfort, constriction and psychological distress for

This long-and-low posture, as it is called, should be continued in the warm-up and for rehabilitation in trot and canter which demand more effort from the horse. However, care should be taken in these gaits not to simply allow the horse to go on his forehand. The rider should, with mind, seat and legs, ask and expect the horse to bring his hindquarters and legs underneath him and raise his back, balancing horizontally on a long, loose rein as shown here, whilst maintaining a stretching, head-down posture

the horse. Constricting the head and neck actually stiffens and hampers the muscles of the whole forehand which, apart from moving the body, are responsible for absorbing concussion in motion. Therefore, the horse can end up with pain from being jarred and sore as well as from abused muscles and related tissues.

The horse *should* be encouraged to send his energy forwards from the hindquarters but into a hand or bit contact which receives and controls it without being hard, rigid and forceful, some would say bullying. In this way, the horse is able to concentrate on the job in hand rather than on his discomfort and to learn to go effectively in whatever way is needed for the task.

The reasons the front of the face should be in front of the vertical, or maybe just on it in the case of advanced horses, are:

- So as to not interfere with the horse's vision. The horse has a narrow, horizontal band of sharp vision, often called the 'visual streak', which he moves to where it is required by means of the movements of his head. By forcing the head carriage behind the vertical, the rider is effectively preventing the horse seeing where he is going.
- So as to not restrict the airflow through the throat. The more oxygen a horse needs to take in and the more carbon dioxide he needs to breathe out, the more open and unrestricted he needs his windpipe to be. The windpipe in a galloping horse, with his naturally extended posture of the head and neck, accommodates this, but a horse whose windpipe is cramped or 'kinked' by the rider but who is still expected to work hard (as do many dressage horses and show jumpers) necessitating good airflow, will find it hard to breathe freely. Their performance and willingness, and certainly their comfort, could all be adversely affected.
- So that the nuchal ligament, which runs from the top of the skull to the withers and beyond, plus other soft tissues in the neck and poll area are not over-stretched and injured by this artificial, strained posture, resulting in tension, pain and possible reluctance to work freely or allow the head to be handled. The tension and pain can extend down the shoulders and along the back resulting in stiffness and lack of free, swinging movement, in a concave rather than convex back and in trailing rather than engaged hindlegs.
- So that the horse's comfort and natural balance can be maintained and he is therefore able to carry the rider much more easily without using his muscles artificially to bear the weight under an enforced posture.

There are occasions when a horse may be asked to go with his head and neck down and with the face a little behind the vertical in order to stretch and supple the tissues *for a few seconds*, particularly the muscles, of the neck and back. This should only be done under the supervision of a knowledgeable and sensitive trainer or rider. In performance rather than gymnastic training the nose should never be brought behind the vertical, as is stressed in the best and most respected books on schooling and which are available for anyone to read. Some titles are given in the Reading List at the end of this book.

Another incorrect way of going often seen which is just as damaging to the horse's physique is with the back down, the head up, neck hollowed and the hindlegs trailing out behind. This is the exact opposite of how the horse should go and puts a considerable amount of strain on the horse's spine from the neck all the way down to the hindquarters. The main cause of this is riders who hang on to the bit and/or pull hard and backwards and/or bang about on the horse's back and ride out of balance, often with a hard seat and stiff legs.

In between these two damaging and ugly ways of going is the right one – with the horse going in a smoothly rounded, engaged outline, back up, quarters and hindlegs under, neck pushed up from the base and forward with the nose in front of the vertical, the horse swinging along freely with correct muscle use and a happy attitude to his work.

This way of going constitutes bodywork under saddle and is not only the means to the end but also the end in itself. It may sound like a rider's Utopia for those who understand how important it is to aspire to it, but it is not an impossible dream. Here's how to do it.

The technique

First of all, you will find in the Reading List at the end of this book several recommended titles on the techniques of riding, because this book is not a riding or schooling manual. I will give below, though, the basic techniques you need to master for your riding and those which will help you to attain the correct posture and way of going in your horse.

1. You need to adopt a properly balanced (classical) seat in the saddle for your flat work. Seen from the side, you should be able to drop an imaginary, perfectly vertical line from a rider's ear, through the shoulder, through the hip *and elbows* (which should rest at the hip, not several inches in front of them), and through the ankle bone.
2. You need to learn to feel your two seat bones which are the lowest bones of your pelvis and to sit lightly on them. (Do not sit on your buttocks and do not sit heavily.) To do this, you have to completely relax and 'let go' with the muscles of your seat and legs.
3. Your posture should comprise a slightly raised breastbone and slightly braced or toned back muscles so that you can sit erect and 'held', imperceptibly holding yourself back from your horse's head and neck. Your upper arms should drop down vertically between your shoulders and hips and, similarly, should be held in tone, although not stiff, so that your horse cannot 'take' by pulling your arms forwards. Your seatbones should be inclined slightly forward in the saddle (do not hollow your back as it will soon start to ache) and your seat and leg muscles should be loose and relaxed, so that you can feel your horse's back through your seat (which you cannot do with tensed muscles) and can drop your legs down, supporting their weight in the stirrups on the balls of your feet.
4. Finally (thank goodness, I am sure you are thinking!), think of the phrase from the Spanish Riding School – 'up the body, down the weight'. I find it helpful to modify this a little by saying 'up the body, down the legs'. The body means your torso or upper body above the waist. The waist itself should be flexible and able to absorb the horse's movements; think of it as the dividing point between the two halves of your body. Your upper body should normally remain still; your lower body (seat and legs) should drape loosely round the saddle and your horse's sides with open hips.

This may all sound like too much to remember, but give yourself time to practise this balanced, sensitive seat and you will feel much more independent and secure in the saddle. Anything new feels strange at first but becomes second nature if you do it consistently. This is the posture to maintain, in flat work, during walk, sitting trot and canter. In rising trot you will find it helpful to keep your back flat, lean forward slightly *from the hip joints*, not the waist, and carry your shoulders above your knees. Then you can easily perform your rise without bobbing up and down by simply tilting the bottom part of your pelvis (the seat bones and pubic bone) forwards instead of pushing yourself up by the legs, and sitting again, with your bottom tucked slightly under, in a 'forward-sit-forward-sit' action rather than an up and down one.

The reason I have stressed this seat is because riding correctly, usually centrally and in balance with the horse makes it easier for him, and for you to give the aids needed to ask him to go into a comfortably firm but sensitive contact, raise his back and bring his hind end under.

You also need to be familiar with the concept of riding 'inside leg into outside rein'. The main purposes of the two reins and the rider's legs are as follows:

- *The outside rein* (the rein nearest the outside of a circle or bend or the fence of the manège) is used to control the speed, to guide and control the bend on turns and circles and to set the horse a given amount of room within which to carry his head and neck at any particular gait. He usually needs to have a gentle and consistent but unmistakable feel on the outside rein, a sort of firm but comfortable 'hand-holding' sort of contact. We are not talking here of horses capable of going in correct self-carriage on the weight of the rein.
- *The inside rein* is used to 'talk' to the horse by means of squeezing movements or little vibrations from the fingers when some adjustment to his 'feel' or carriage is required, to invite him round bends by being held sideways into the bend and to gently but unmistakably operate a feel-and-release contact on the bit to encourage the horse to 'give' or flex to the bit by relaxing his lower jaw and tongue and flexing at the poll.
- *The outside leg* guides the horse around bends and asks for lateral movements and also for canter if the rider is using diagonal aids (i.e. left leg asks for right canter and vice versa).
- *The inside leg* asks for energy, impulsion and forward movement and acts as a support 'pillar' during turns and circles.

The idea of riding inside leg into outside rein means that the inside leg asks for the energy and the outside rein contains it so that it does not, in equestrian parlance, all escape out of the front end. If you keep the outside rein contact steady and moderately firm but slightly elastic in the early stages (becoming lighter as the horse's carriage becomes established), the horse will have a comfortable but clear border or limit to work up to.

To get him to work within that space which you have given him, that is, the length of the outside rein, you need to keep the contact on the outside rein and tap or squeeze intermittently with the inside leg inwards and sideways immediately behind the girth. At the same time, you alternately feel and release down the inside rein, firmly but sensitively, so that the horse feels an intermittent pressure on his inside lower jaw and tongue asking him to relax them and flex at the poll.

Start this way:

It helps if you have taught your horse the 'head down' request described earlier. Have him in his bridle and stand on one side of him, say the right, at the halt. Hold the reins in the normal riding way, the left rein with your left hand which becomes the outside rein, and the right rein with your right hand which becomes the inside rein. Take an even contact, gentle but there, on both reins, keep the left one steady and feel and release on the inside one, saying 'head down'. If the horse resists, lower the inside hand a little and repeat the feel-and-release movement, maybe a *little* firmer, till the horse gets the idea. It may help to have a rider on board tapping immediately behind the girth with the inside leg, as described.

The *instant* the horse relaxes his jaw, flexes at the poll and drops his head a little, let the inside rein go loose (and stop the leg aid), praise him with 'good boy' and stroke his neck. Do this procedure once more from the right side, then twice from the left, to establish it, then mount and do the same thing from the saddle in halt.

With horses who are very resistant or stiff in the jaw, it helps to give them a titbit immediately before you start this work to get the mouth moving. An assistant can also insert a finger immediately below the bit and tickle the tongue, which almost always results in movement.

The rewards of stopping the aids (fingers and leg) plus 'good boy' are most important. If the horse obeys but you continue to ask, he cannot know that he has responded as you wished. The praise keeps good feeling about the training process and most horses regard it as a reward. This is a good basis for all schooling.

Move off into walk and keep your outside rein contact, tap with your inside leg and feel and release sensitively but significantly with your inside rein, lowering it slightly if necessary, and say 'head down'. Progress to trot, sitting or rising, and continue with this technique – remembering always to be very quick and consistent in your praise, stopping the aids and saying 'good boy', immediately when the horse complies.

The horse, to use his muscles properly, must gradually get into the habit of going with his head down and his lower jaw relaxed during much of his time under saddle. The main schooling gait is trot but the same technique can be used in canter, using the 'feel' on the moment of suspension and releasing the inside rein with the fingers as the leading leg lands.

Once you and the horse are used to this technique, at the moment you release or lessen the inside rein contact in response to his flexing, softening and lowering the head, ask with your inside leg for him to go forward into this posture, keeping it light and energetic but controlling the speed (which must not be too fast) with your outside rein. This will give you impulsion and lift and aid correct muscle development. You should be able to feel his back rise and the energy pushing forwards and up beneath your seat.

Once the horse is going well, thrusting from and engaged behind, with his back up and his head down, jaw flexed and light in hand, *praise him and stop the aids – just enjoy what he is giving you. This is what it is all about. This is the way to achieve a reactive, light and well-developed horse.* If you keep asking him for what he is already doing he will become resentful, confused, heavy in sides and mouth and possibly difficult because he doesn't understand what more he can do. In truth, he can do nothing more because he is already doing what you have asked for!

You need to use your judgement and patience and only expect a few strides at a time if this work (and it *is* muscular work) is new to the horse. Over the weeks, he will be able to maintain his posture for longer and improve his self-carriage. Because it is physically tiring, most horses will not push themselves in the way a human athlete will or someone working out in the gym. Therefore, you have to demand a little more and a little more otherwise the muscles will not develop in response to the stress of work. Be very tactful and work up from a few strides to, say, a full 20m circle, in two or three weeks, schooling for half an hour three or four days a week and in short spells out hacking. Hacking is also the ideal opportunity to let your horse really walk out on a loose rein, conditions permitting. It is extremely easy to wreck the walk by never letting the horse walk out freely, his head, neck, back and tail all swinging in rhythm.

When schooling, do not work your horse for more than a very few minutes at a time per session, say five minutes, depending on his fitness because:

1. You do not want him to associate schooling with hard, long spells of drilling and psychological domination or he will become bitter, resigned or will start to play up, depending on his temperament. Great tact and ready rewards are needed.
2. Give your horse plenty of breaks sitting light and walking on a *loose, free* rein with the buckle on the withers, so that the muscles which have been contracting and held in tone can relax and allow the blood, lymph and energy to flow freely through their loose tissues.

3. Remember that just standing still with the head down is mentally rewarding and physically beneficial, after a spell of muscular work.

4. Remember also that horses not allowed to rest very frequently, relax, recover and stretch *during* schooling sessions experience pain in the form of aching and possibly cramp in their muscles. The muscles stiffen, harden and can become injured and go into long-term spasm, none of which you want.

The work of developing the correct muscles will be greatly aided by three techniques:

1. Perform transitions (with the head down as described above) not only from gait to gait but also within gaits, from shortened to lengthened strides and back again within the horse's current balance and ability, always asking for correct muscle use.

2. Work over poles in all gaits, graduating up to six poles. As the horse progresses with the poles, raise the ends, most easily with wooden, brick-sized blocks or plastic jump wings with low pole grooves.

3. Work up and down hills, gentle slopes at first and steeper ones as the horse becomes stronger. Horses like to get their heads down going up hill to bring the weight forward and up so give them their heads. A little encouragement will soon show a stiff horse the way. Going downhill, the hind end will come under and the head and neck will *not* rise much but be about horizontal.

Basic work over poles is good for getting the horse to look down where he is going, to thrust from the hind end, to spring and lift and to raise the back. The rider should sit lightly

Here Tracey and Cyril are walking through the Tellington maze (more information is given later on this). Tracey is using an exaggerated open and light inside rein and has her inside seatbone very well forward, supporting with the outside leg slightly back and the outside rein 'pushing' Cyril around the turn by means of sideways pressure just in front of the withers. These aids enable Cyril, without any force or coercion, to negotiate the maze with flexion and bend, which he does easily. Aids which do actually help the horse as opposed to try to force him (the word 'aid' meaning 'help', of course) are vital to good and correct muscle development. If the horse is fighting or resisting the rider, this sort of muscle development will not happen but development of the wrong muscles will. This is why it is so easy to tell, just by looking at a horse, whether or not he is well ridden

Yvonne Yates and her part-Arab endurance gelding, Fred, before classical training. Yvonne has quite short stirrups and tends to sit on her buttocks instead of her seatbones which causes an incorrect balance. Partly due to this, although she has light hands and a loose rein, Fred goes in all gaits with his back down and his head up (note the standing martingale to keep the head down) which is not an effective or comfortable way to carry weight. Long-term, it can also lead to back and joint problems. She is also using roundings with the pelham bit which does not get the best out of a pelham as it is not possible to differentiate between the curb and snaffle actions (Photo: Peter Orr)

Regarding the pole work, experiment, with the help of a friend on the ground, to find your horse's individual stride length so that you can place them accordingly. Later, you can widen and narrow the distances between them slightly to develop adaptability in your horse's gaits. For a riding horse about 16hh high, poles for walk could be set initially at about 2ft 3in or 67cm. For trot try them at about 3ft 3in or 1m and for canter at about 11ft or 3.3m. Give him a longish rein and do not try to influence his stride when you are trying to discover his natural length. Ask him to go over one pole first to tell him what is happening. Then try two poles, then three and so on because the horse may trip and even fall until you find his distance and until he is used to this work. If the distances are too narrow he will hit the poles and if they are too wide he will stretch too much or put in extra little strides. You need to feel an easy gait with a little more thrust and lift, but almost as if the poles were not there.

Gymnastic jumping over grids of little jumps and cross poles is also beneficial and many horses enjoy going loose down a jumping lane.

A fourth technique not available to everyone is to walk your horse in water. The water should be no deeper than just up to the horse's knees, shallower than this to start with. This is just the right depth to develop muscles as the horse lifts his legs up out of the water but not so deep as to cause strain. (Deep 'water walks' are used in hydrotherapy, under expert supervision.) The cold of the water is also beneficial to the legs and feet. The ground beneath the water must be sound and safe, not boggy or stony. Most horses naturally put their heads down when walking in water (and some like to roll!) and a racehorse trainer once told me that he considered a half mile walk in water equivalent to a mile's gallop. It is hard work and also develops the horse's cardiovascular system as well as his muscles.

After only a few classical lessons, plus using classical techniques in between lessons – most important - Yvonne has a slightly longer stirrup, a better-balanced seat with the emphasis on the seatbones and better use of the pelham by using two pairs of reins. Her hands are better positioned (thumbs on top) which gives a more sensitive feel and use of the reins) and she shows the classic straight line from her elbow, through her hand to the horse's mouth. Fred is reaching forward and down with his back and belly up and the standing martingale, although still present, is superfluous. Yvonne said that his co-operation and attitude also improved (Photo: Peter Orr)

In addition to correct posture and muscle development in 'straight' work, the horse needs to perform lateral work in order to develop the muscles responsible for moving his body sideways and producing an all-over, balanced musculature.

The best exercises for this are, initially, leg yielding, shoulder out and shoulder in, first on the straight and later on turns and circles. Any book on good riding technique will give details on how to do these schooling movements and a good teacher will teach you how to do them *without coercion*, using your seat and body aids, including weight.

The most beneficial gait in which to do them, for muscle development, is the walk because in this gait the muscles are weight-bearing most of the time as the horse moves laterally so he has to push against the ground in order to move sideways. In trot, most of the 'travel' takes place in the air during the moment of suspension. Walking these exercises is actually harder work for the horse but it gives both him and the rider time to think about what they are doing.

I hope this section on Riding will help you to realise how important and beneficial correct schooling is and will give you a good idea of how to go on with or without a sympathetic, knowledgeable teacher. I hope also that the books in the Reading List will give you further food for thought.

SECTION 4
THERAPIES

The techniques in this section are regarded more as therapies than as management techniques such as grooming although there is inevitably a link between the two. It cannot be too strongly advised that, before trying to apply an actual therapy to your horse, expert advice should be taken from a veterinary surgeon and a trained therapist. Both of these two types of professionals will understand that you would like to help your own horse as much as possible and should be willing to help you acquire basic techniques to apply yourself, or at least check what you read in this and other books.

There are certain situations when touch-type therapies should not be used. Great care has to be used in applying, for instance, shiatsu, massage and aromatherapy to pregnant mares, and horses suffering from a disease such as influenza, strangles or others will not want to be handled any more than necessary. Injured horses, likewise, may not benefit from some therapies such as stretches, some aspects of physiotherapy or others.

Always be very ready to consult the experts and go by their advice whilst knowing your own horse and learning as much as you can yourself.

AROMATHERAPY

Many people find it difficult to accept that a scent or smell can have a therapeutic effect on the body or mind. If we look at it another way, we must all have experienced the effects (therapeutic or otherwise) that aromas can have on us. Liking or disliking a particular perfume is one example. Classic though it may be, not everyone likes the smell of, for instance, Chanel No. 5. The effect that a welcome or unwelcome smell has on us is just a very basic example of what aromas can do. If we are driving along in our cars in a country district and a really repulsive smell comes through the air system or windows (probably 'fertilizer'!), we usually pull a face, say 'Pooh!' or something stronger and, in some cases particularly if the smell lingers, start to feel sick. The smell of rotten flesh or bad eggs make most people feel nauseous (the Chemistry Lab at school used to make me feel that way which may be why I was never particularly good at Chemistry) but the mingled scents of a cottage garden on a warm, sunny day must make most people feel – well, indescribably wonderful.

Scents can have a stimulating effect (such as mint or rosemary) or a calming one (such as lavender or jasmine), so there is no doubt that aromas as common as all those mentioned, 'good' or 'bad', clearly do have a physical effect on us (nausea, stimulation, calming) and a mental one (uplifted, carefree, exhilarated) in that we feel bad or good when we experience them.

But actual therapy? Can it really be? Presumably if you had eaten something which really did not agree with you and you needed to be sick, a smell triggering nausea and perhaps vomiting would be regarded as therapeutic after a fashion because it would rid you of the root

93

of your problem which should always be the aim of any healing whenever possible. Perhaps it could be felt, also, that any aroma which relaxed you would consequently reduce or banish the effects of stress, trauma and anxiety (which themselves can cause actual physical and mental disorders such as gastric ulcers or psychosis) and so could surely be regarded as therapeutic.

Historically, ancient civilisations have used aromas to treat recognised mental and physical diseases. It is known that some essential oils (which form the basis of modern aromatherapy) have anti-bacterial and anti-viral properties and some have other types of healing properties, encouraging the body to heal itself (for example, lavender oil is good for healing skin injuries and diseases as well as many other conditions). In the late nineteenth century, René-Maurice Gattefosse (whose name probably appears in just about every book on aromatherapy) did much research work on the qualities and uses of essential oils.

In common with many other 'natural' or non-synthetic medicines and therapies, the middle of the twentieth century saw a decline in their general use because of the development of synthetic drugs. Many of these were chemically similar to their natural counterparts but it was felt by researchers that simply taking the active ingredients of the natural substance and recreating the chemical structure of that part only would be more effective and would increase affordability and availability. Many health-care professionals interested in complementary therapies feel that this unbalances the end product and is what brings about additional, unwanted effects (which we call side-effects). Also, they do not, many therapists believe, contain the natural energy or life force of naturally sourced products. There is also the problem, with antibiotics, of their becoming less effective as the bacteria and viruses breed new generations resistant to them.

Essential oils

What does this phrase mean? Essential oils are ones which are volatile at room temperature, that is, they evaporate rapidly producing a vapour or gas without chemical change in the molecular structure. Non-essential oils such as the 'base' oils which are used as carriers for

A small selection of essential oils plus a larger bottle of base oil, all in dark glass bottles to protect them from light, plus a small ceramic dish for mixing the oils

most essential oils do not do this. Essential oils are almost always diluted in base oils because of their volatility and also because they are too 'strong' to use neat directly on the skin although they can be inhaled. Two oils which many therapists say can be used without dilution are tea tree (or ti tree) oil and lavender oil. I have certainly never had problems when using these two oils undiluted. Others with this property are yarrow, seaweed and German chamomile. Roman chamomile must be diluted.

Essential oils are found in various parts of plants and, due to the differences in the plants' tissues, have to be extracted by different means such as distillation, cold pressing or straightforward crushing. The end result is available in organic form (the most expensive) or inorganic, in little brown bottles with a plastic distributor in the neck which gives one drop at a time, for that is how essential oils are measured in use, or by millilitres (ml). They are available from specialist suppliers and through most health shops and some chemists. Professional therapists of various disciplines also often sell them, along with other remedies and products such as herbal products, homoeopathic remedies, flower remedies and so on.

What conditions are oils used for?

Probably most people first think of massage when aromatherapy is mentioned. For horses, oils can also be inhaled and massage and inhalation are the two main ways in which they are used although a few drops of appropriate oil can be added to hot or cold water in which a compress is soaked and applied to, for example, an injured leg. Administration by mouth (by licking the hand or in the feed) is also possible if your therapist or vet agrees.

Essential oils have traditionally been used to treat many conditions from infections to allergies plus diseases of degeneration and wear and tear. A few examples would be arthritis, respiratory disease, RAO (recurrent airway obstruction or 'broken wind') laminitis, skin disorders, wounds and sprains, aches and pains after strenuous work, immune disease disorders, emotional, psychological and behavioural disorders, and digestive problems.

How does it work?

As always experts disagree! The oils, or rather the fragrant molecules (which are actual physical particles) are said to be absorbed through the skin when massaged into it but some believe that the amount of product actually absorbed will be low because the thickness of skin (as opposed to the mucous membranes in the nose and lungs) hampers absorption. When applied via inhalation through the mucous membranes of the nose, the molecules have an effect on the limbic system, a group of structures sited towards the front of the brain concerned with detecting smells and believed to be involved in certain aspects of behaviour such as the generation and control of emotions. The molecules can also be absorbed into the bloodstream from the lungs and be circulated around the body.

The sense of smell in the horse is closely linked to that of taste and is highly developed, as with all herbivorous mammals. It is used to assess food, in recognition of herd members, in bonding mare and foal, in detecting the presence of predators or anything unpleasant and to be avoided (such as worming medicines) and in breeding, when stallions can infallibly detect much better and quicker than man when a mare is full in season and ready for mating. Horses also clearly recognise humans by smell and sight as well as sound, and familiar smells permeate a horsebox when a horse is travelling and tell him that he is nearly home.

Domesticated, stabled horses may have had their ability to detect and differentiate between different scents severely restricted by the very many smells around a domestic stable yard. When buying scent for yourself in the perfumery department of your local department store, you will probably be advised not to test more than three perfumes at one time because more than this will lessen the effectiveness of your sense of smell. Consider, then, what the horse's nose is bombarded with every day – feeds with flavourings and 'attractive' smells added to them, shampoos, coat dressings, washes, medicines, plastics, the artificial smells on people such as deodorants, hair products, talcum powder and so on and the exhaust fumes of traffic in and around the stable yard. Horses out at grass are better off but are bound to experience fumes from traffic in many situations. They can smell the different grasses and plants (which helps them to decide what to eat in the first place) and can sniff out medicinal plants for whatever condition is currently affecting them – if the plants are growing in their paddock, of course. There is much to be said for incorporating a general herb strip in paddocks for this purpose.

When the horse breathes in scent-laden air, it passes up his nostrils carrying with it the tiny particles or molecules of various aromas. These are dissolved on the moist, fine mucous membranes lining the nasal area and also come into contact with a structure here called Jacobson's Organ or the vomeronasal organ via ducts in the roof of the horse's mouth. When a horse closes off his nostrils by raising his upper lip in the gesture called *flehmen*, it is believed that he is closely assessing scents with this organ. Olfactory nerves (those used in the sense of smell) pass messages to structures in the brain, informing it what kind of smell is present.

Safety

Because essential oils are chemically structured substances, it would be foolish to think that they are harmless. They can be very potent and some of them can be toxic. They can also have unwanted effects if the wrong oils are used. If a person or animal is sensitive or allergic to a particular chemical substance, an essential oil with a similar molecular structure can also cause a sensitivity reaction. Some oils can cause effects similar to sunburn if areas massaged with them are then exposed to strong ultra violet light (such as full sun or a sun bed). For these reasons, it is always wisest to at least initially use essential oils and aromatherapy in conjunction with the advice of a trained, qualified aromatherapist, until you learn more yourself.

The oils can be administered by letting the horse lick them off your hand but may then be regarded as medicines. In some countries, a veterinary surgeon would need to be consulted before this route of administration could be used. As most vets are not trained in aromatherapy, the therapist and vet would probably need to consult before advising this method. An owner may do more to his or her horse than a therapist, but should also check with his or her veterinary surgeon about the safety or otherwise of any oil proposed for use in this way.

How effective are essential oils?

Again, opinions vary but a general opinion may be that oils can cure some actual illnesses some of the time. The oils can have antimicrobial, pharmacological and anti-stress properties but in many cases there is no proof available which is acceptable to the orthodox scientific community although research continues. This applies to most complementary therapies. The term 'anecdotal evidence' has come to be a derogatory one in terms of scientific proof of efficacy but thousands of years of documentation, record-keeping, practical use and traditional training cannot be pointless, in the view of many including this author.

Because a little knowledge is often a dangerous thing, a trained, qualified therapist should be consulted initially, but the owner can certainly carry on the good work and acquire a useful working knowledge of aromatherapy.

Choosing the oils

On a therapist's first visit, he or she will take a thorough record of the horse's type, behaviour, physical condition, background and what problems the owner perceives in his behaviour, performance and health. Based on this and her detailed knowledge of oils, she will then select possibly one to five oils which she considers likely to be helpful, and offer them one by one to the horse, allowing him to take his time although most horses are quick decision-makers. The horse's own choice is crucial as the wrong oil (one the horse instinctively knows he does not want or need) can sometimes have adverse effects. If the horse shows interest, this is noted and perhaps another oil chosen as well, if the therapist thinks a blend of more than one will be appropriate.

The way to offer the oils is to hold the small bottle well down in the hand so that its top with the plastic distributor is level with the finger and thumb. If it protrudes the horse may well try to take it, like a titbit, and if he can get hold of it at all this may result in broken glass and an injury. As the oils will be undiluted, the therapist will make sure that the bottle does not touch the horse's skin.

The horse will smell the oil with first one nostril (and sometimes this is enough) and then the other. If he looks interested and keeps smelling the oil and even tries to lick the top of the bottle, he clearly could benefit from this one. He may also perform the *flehmen* reaction, flare his nostrils or try to come towards the therapist if she moves away a little.

Other oils are offered in the same way and a note made of which he likes. Usually, the oils he prefers most predominate in a blend, with smaller amounts of others. If the horse turns away, do not pursue the matter: he does not want or need that particular oil and his judgement must be trusted.

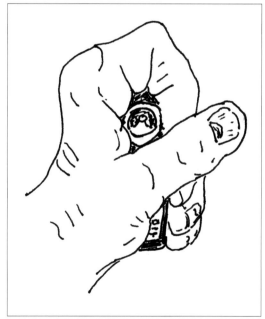

Hold the bottle well down inside the hand so that the horse cannot bite it, and offer it to the horse without touching his nostrils

Keep a record yourself of which oils he likes and which he rejects so that you can follow his treatment and carry on whatever the therapist recommends. Because oils can have not only one direct effect but also a balancing effect, particularly with emotional issues, it may be found that the same oil may be used for extremes of the same problem. The essential oil of rose is

97

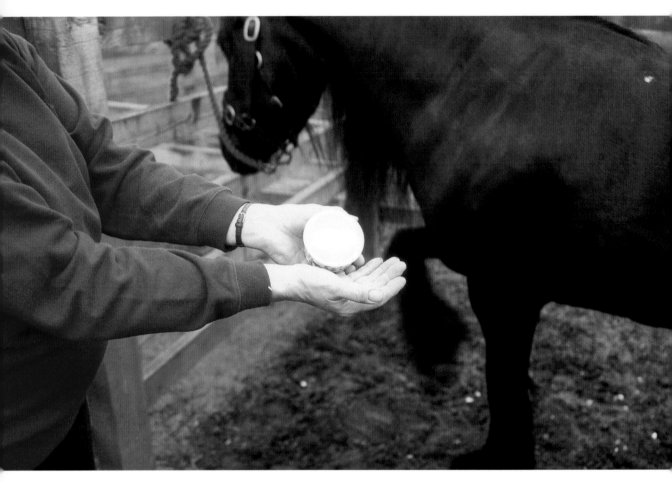

Mix the oils in your dish and pour the mixture into your hand

particularly useful in that it can help both mares and stallions in breeding, either stimulating interest and even normal cycling but also calming down excessively sexual reactions. Lavender is a multi-use oil which can be used to heal physical wounds and injuries but also calm and also uplift the emotions. For this reason, often other beneficial side-effects may be noted as well as the one principally wanted.

Qualities of oils

You may have heard of perfumes and essential oils as having 'top', 'middle' and 'bottom' notes in their scents. The expression 'top note' means that the aroma/oil will be very noticeable and will evaporate very quickly in air; 'middle note' means that it is not so obvious in smell and will evaporate more slowly and so last a little longer; 'base note' is the term applied to oils which take the longest time to evaporate, which are even less obvious in smell but which last the longest.

Often, for both practical and therapeutic purposes, a blend of all three will be effective. The qualities of oils can vary according to the time of season during which they are harvested and even the time of day, like new mown grass cut for hay or haylage. The scents of oils can vary considerably although the chemical structure will not.

As mentioned earlier, the quality of the oil as to whether it is organic or inorganic makes a difference to its purity and price. As aromatherapy becomes more and more popular, some retailers appear to have been sourcing essential oils from suppliers producing less 'pure' oils for reasons of commercial economy and these oils may be found in such retail outlets as supermarkets, beauty shops, hairdressers and so on. The author feels that it is best to buy organic oils from a reputable source such as a health food store or, ideally, from a qualified aromatherapist or other complementary health professional such as a medical herbalist.

Applying the oils

You will need your own home kit of base oils or gels and essential oils. As you become more experienced you will be able to add to your preliminary kit.

(You may well be asked by friends and other owners to 'treat' their horses and ponies but, depending on which country you live in, you may well be breaking the law. Always recommend them to a vet and/or qualified aromatherapist.)

Base oils are those in which essential oils are diluted and may be, among others, sweet almond oil, jojoba, grapeseed, walnut and apricot kernel oil. Aloe vera gel is also an excellent base for carrying essential oils and has healing properties of its own; it is also useful where base oils cannot be used such as in cases of irritated skin. Grapeseed and sweet almond are very light oils which will not leave an oily deposit where they have been applied or massaged in whereas jojoba oil is heavier. Oils which are absorbed well and quickly are apricot kernel and walnut.

A good basic home kit of oils may be as follows but be sure to consult both your therapist and your vet before giving oils orally. Only the main traditional qualities of each oil are given.

- *Tea tree:* multi-healing and good for fungal skin infections such as ringworm, for thrush in the feet, for skin wounds and insect bites. Orally it may be used for urinary problems. May be used undiluted.
- *Lavender:* another multi-healer, lavender is particularly good for wounds, burns, and those which are slow to heal. It also helps prevent scarring. It is said to help with immune system problems and is calming and relaxing. May be used undiluted.
- *Yarrow:* good for wounds, having anti-inflammatory and anti-bacterial properties. Also good for rashes and itchy skin disorders, insect bites and urinary disorders. Helps 'release' powerful, adverse emotions such as anger, loneliness, insecurity. May be used undiluted.
- *Rosemary:* good to inhale before a schooling session or competition as it aids concentration. It stimulates circulation so is good for horses on reduced exercise due to box rest. Helps with muscular aches, spasmodic colic.
- *Peppermint:* Mentally stimulating and uplifting so good for overly laid-back horses. Good for aches and strains of work. Anti-inflammatory and pain-killing effects. Stimulates and soothes digestion and helps to clear air passages being generally good for respiratory problems.
- *Eucalyptus:* again helps respiratory problems.

- *Rose:* helps balance female sexual/oestrus problems. Good for horses having suffered previous abuse.
- *Vetiver:* good for tense, nervous and highly-strung horses as is said to be 'grounding', calming and relaxing.

Your therapist will be able to help you with blending oils as this is quite an art, but you will get used to your own horse's needs in this respect. The oils are highly concentrated and sometimes expensive so often only two or three drops are needed to as little as a teaspoon or dessertspoonful of essential oil for application to one site, or around the nostrils or (very gently) up the throat for inhalation. A body massage of certain areas will necessitate more base oil and, obviously, more drops of essential oil, but an economical way to use your blend for massage is to rub it on your hands and then on the horse. In this way you eliminate waste but still achieve your effects.

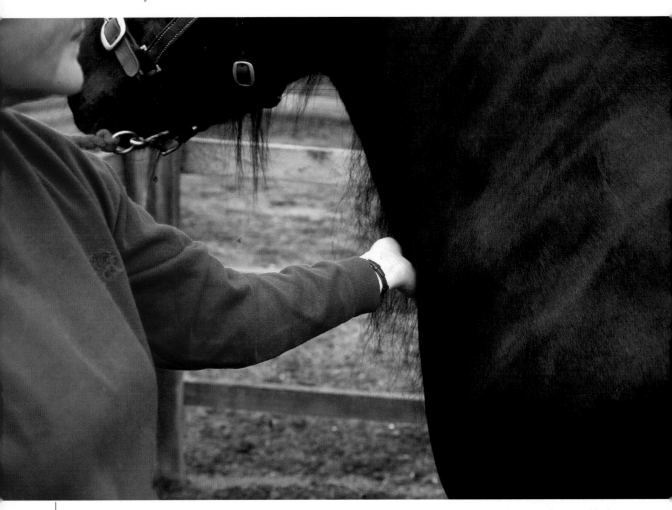

Rub the oil gently into the area required so that it reaches the skin. This mix containing eucalyptus is being rubbed on Rose's throat to help with her breathing

Storage

Oils (essential and base) come in dark glass bottles, dark because exposure to light damages them and changes their chemical structure and glass because it is an inert substance with no active properties of its own and cannot damage your oils. All oils must be stored in a cool, dark, locked cupboard to provide them with protective conditions and prevent others, particularly children, having access to them. They should be treated like medicines. Keep the tops screwed firmly on to prevent evaporation. Oils may last between six months to five years or so when stored properly, the lighter oils for the shorter periods and vice versa. Check the quality, clarity and scent of oils you have had for a while and consult your therapist if in doubt.

Remember:

- When working with your oils in the stable yard, it is best to store them upright in a proper compartmentalised box, made for the purpose, with a lockable lid.
- When working on the horse, offering oils to him or applying them, close the lid properly and if there are children or dogs loose lock it.
- Do not take it into the stable in case the horse treads on it.
- Do not stand bottles on ledges or even on the ground in case they fall or are broken or trodden on.
- Do not leave tops off, either.
- Do not let people borrow the oils to try on their own horse.
- Remember that they are medicines.
- Take the key home with you.
- Either take the box home, preferably, or lock it in a cupboard or locker in your bay or area of your livery yard with your first aid kit. Even if someone else has access to your first aid supplies in case your horse has an accident in your absence, they should not have access to your aromatherapy box.

Applying oils to the body

In the section of this book on Massage, you will read details of the procedure called effleurage which is the most useful method for applying oils. It is basically specialised stroking and can be mastered with a little practise. Combining the oils with a massage is doubly beneficial. Normally, the oils should be massaged in with the lie of the hair but some masseurs and aromatherapists prefer to massage towards the heart during a body massage.

Applications for a specific purpose may be made to particular areas. It may be recommended that behavioural, attitude and emotional problems such as depression, 'vices' or stereotypies, an unwilling attitude, aggression, insecurity and so on should be treated by applying the appropriate blend to the top (dorsal) part of the neck and the poll area whereas the lower (ventral) part of the neck and the chest, where the windpipe and gullet run, may be used for, for instance, respiratory problems. This area is avoided in massage itself because of the windpipe and gullet, so oils must be applied very carefully here. In cases of colic, the blend should be applied to the thin skin under the belly and between the hind legs. Obviously, application at the site of a problem should be used in such cases as insect bites, nettle rash, wounds, bruises, mud fever, sweet itch, arthritis, sprains and so on. Do not apply an oil direct

101

to an open wound unless your therapist has said that this is acceptable. Base oils, in any case, may prevent healing so aloe vera gel would be a better alternative.

Inhalations can be direct from a correctly held bottle or can be prepared with very hot water and offered to the horse from a proper nose-bag (often available from carriage-driving harness suppliers) or a non-plastic sack. Put a layer of hay in the bottom and sprinkle in about ten to fifteen drops of your oil, possibly eucalyptus, pour in about half a litre or a pint of very hot water, then add another thin layer of hay to diffuse the steam, and let your horse inhale it *as he wishes*. I should certainly not fasten the bag or sack on his head or to his headcollar as he then has no choice in the matter. Here again, the command 'head down' can be very useful. Let him inhale carefully for about five minutes then take everything away and dispose of it in the rubbish. This can be done three or four times a day.

Giving the oils by mouth (first having checked with your vet and/or therapist) can be directly on the feed (say five to seven drops in the feed twice a day) or the horse can lick the blend from your hand, usually with the underside of his tongue.

Oils may 'work' quickly within a day or less, or it may take a week or so for any improvement to be noticed. With any of the above administrations, keep in touch with your therapist and discontinue use if there is no improvement after two weeks. If you have any adverse reactions such as a deterioration in the condition, a skin reaction such as soreness or swelling, stop using the oils and consult your vet or therapist.

If your horse develops a dislike of any particular oil or blend, again take professional advice until you feel able to handle it yourself. If an oil is no longer liked (needed) by the horse it may be that it has done its job and should be discontinued. On the other hand, his condition may have changed and a different oil or blend may be needed.

Aromatherapy is one of those practices which can be extremely rewarding and pleasant for both horse and owner and one which I find helpful and reassuring, and quite effective, truly complementing other forms of healing, orthodox and 'natural'.

HYDROTHERAPY

Hydrotherapy simply means 'water therapy'. Water as a means of healing physical injuries in horses and as a means of getting them fit is far from new. The benefits comprise not only the cold of the water which helps to allay inflammation (heat, swelling and consequent pain) but also the pressure of the water on swollen tissues and, where there are problems of action in the horse or where specific muscle development is needed, the very action of lifting the legs out of the water.

I was lucky enough to learn to ride on the Fylde beach in Lancashire and walking and, at that time, playing on ponies in the sea was just a part of life – not to mention climbing up the sandhills and sliding down the other side which the ponies seemed to love. When I was older and competing I was made aware of the benefits of walking horses knee-deep in the sea – the cold was excellent for the tendons and ligaments and the work built up not only muscles but also cardiovascular fitness. The horses were really blowing after a half-mile wade in the sea. Then as they blew less and less you had a good idea of how fit they were; no one used pulse rates or heart rate monitors in those days because it was never thought of and monitors had not been invented for general use on equine athletes.

Certainly one of the most famous racehorses in the world, triple Grand National winner, Red Rum, was trained on the beach at Southport, Merseyside, by his trainer, Ginger McCain, to

Horses who swim well use a diagonal motion with the legs like this, but others may use a random, erratic movement which does not benefit their physique. The horse also unavoidably holds his body in exactly the wrong posture required for either ridden or driven work, with the head and neck stretched up and the back down. Clearly, this does not make for development or maintenance of the correct muscles for work. If the horse is unused to swimming, this will also cause stress and even muscle pain in addition to the considerable exertion required to swim. If the horse is used to swimming, the wrong muscles will be being developed all the time. Correct, gymnastic work on the flat will be needed to counteract this

Walking horses no deeper than knee- or hock-deep in water with a safe bottom is very beneficial to their development and is exerting enough to also increase the fitness of the cardiovascular system. Many trainers feel that the cold of the water and its pressure on the legs has a dually beneficial effect of helping to allay any heat and provide a light massage of the tissues. The head and neck should be allowed to be extended downwards, which most horses will wish to do, but keep them moving and be alert as many horses like to roll in water, rider and tack notwithstanding!

win his races, having arrived in his yard, I understand, with recurrent soundness problems. It was generally believed that regular paddling in the cold sea after his work-outs on the beach was largely instrumental in restoring him to soundness. Another school of thought is that the salt has a bracing, tightening effect on the skin of horses' legs and salt water is certainly an excellent basic disinfectant for wounds. Unfortunately, the Irish Sea is, I gather, one of the most polluted and radioactive in the world but Red Rum did not seem to suffer from it and lived a long, happy life after he arrived in Southport, the neighbouring beach to where I was brought up.

During the 1960s, my veterinary surgeon advised me to take my horse in the sea, stifle deep, to treat an obstinate wound he had sustained in the field. We did this religiously and it did seem to help more than any other treatment. One summer's evening when the sea was as calm as glass apart from a gentle swell we were standing mesmerised looking out to the horizon and the huge, orange sun, the wound immersed in the salt water, when a dog barking on the beach caused my horse to try to turn quickly. His feet had sunk deep into the wet, soft sand on the sea bed and he could not get them out quickly enough so we both fell in three feet of sea water. The wound healed surely enough but the salt water did not do my saddle any good.

Most people do not have access to the sea, and rivers, streams and ponds have notoriously unsafe bottoms. If you can find water which has both safe access and footing you may well wish to take advantage of paddling in the water even if your horse does not appear to have any kind of unwanted heat in his legs. (The old adage was always that a horse's legs and feet should be as cold as ice.)

The late Gordon Richards, one of Britain's most successful trainers of steeplechasers, had a flowing stream running through his premises at Greystoke Castle, Cumbria, and would regularly stand horses in it as a natural treatment for their legs. He swore to me that it played a big part in keeping them sound and any horse who had even a suspicion of a leg problem would go on the stream régime. Horses would also be stood in it after racing and schooling over fences just as a matter of course.

Commercial facilities

Owners who have difficulty in getting to suitable water may be able to reach a therapy or rehabilitation yard which has a water walk, water whirlpool or other hydrotherapy facility. In natural water sources, probably it is easiest to cope with water which is knee deep as this depth is just deep enough to make the horses work with little risk of their losing their balance and ending up, rider and all, in the drink. Purpose-built water walks can offer varying depths of water, and water which is elbow and stifle deep can be used for horses to wade through as part of a physiotherapy programme. The horses do not even try to lift their legs out of deep water, and the force of using their muscles against the resistance of the water can be very beneficial.

Swimming has been popular for racehorses and competition horses for a few decades now and some owners do swim their horses when they have natural or purpose-built facilities within reasonable reach. Swimming does have definite advantages: it develops and maintains cardiovascular fitness and is a means of maintaining the heart and lungs with work which is, however, weightless and so ideal for horses recovering from leg injuries. The cold and pressure of the water appear to be beneficial in such cases but there are disadvantages which potential users need to be aware of.

1. The owners of commercial facilities usually claim that horses enjoy swimming. Horses are not natural swimmers but, in the wild, they can swim if they have to. Some horses do like swimming and are good swimmers. Many, though, do not like it and some are frightened of it. Also, some do not swim well and if they don't you cannot teach them, of course. At one commercial therapy yard I visited I witnessed clearly frightened horses being bullied and forced into the water and made to swim in the cold water much too far, in my view. One was still shuddering from cold (although by then in a solarium) and distress half an hour after being allowed to come out.
2. From a therapy viewpoint, the best shape of swimming facility is a straight, water-filled passage as the horse can go straight down evenly using the muscles on both sides with relative ease. The more usual type are circular, popular with trainers because the horse can be made to keep going round and round until he has swum his required distance without repeatedly having to be brought out and put back in again. One exit and re-entry, for the purpose of changing direction, is usually enough. Swimming on a constant bend can be very stressful for the horses and, if they are not naturally good swimmers, can create uneven muscle development and possible pain and even cramp, as well as distressing them as they try to stay 'on course' and afloat.
3. Swimming unavoidably puts the horse into exactly the opposite posture to that required for good riding technique and muscle development, with the head and neck stretched up and the back down. Horses unused to this appear to me to find it extremely uncomfortable and hard work: if they are used to it then they are, by definition, developing the wrong muscles for riding as the horse's musculature grows more used to coping with the specific demands made on it by the swimming position. Some physiotherapists, though, do say that this posture should be used as well as its opposite for the sake of putting the joints of the spine (between the vertebrae) through their maximum range of motion every day and to promote even, longitudinal muscle development.

On balance, I should not swim a horse of mine regularly or for long (and not at all if he did not like it) but would gladly use water walks, whirlpools and jacuzzis which massage the legs by means of water jets applying pressure, accompanied by the benefits of cold temperatures on the legs.

If a horse is swum, other therapeutic and rehabilitation exercise should be undertaken to counteract the concave posture necessarily adopted during swimming. In the stable the horse should be fed (concentrates, if given, and fibre such as hay or haylage) from ground level to promote stretching of the top line neck, back and hindquarter muscles and other soft tissues. If sound enough, he should be turned out to graze, when he is automatically in the desired posture. If he cannot be ridden, he should be walked in hand, lunged and long-reined and encouraged to go in this correct posture of 'both ends down and the middle up', and not by being forced into it by training aids or gadgets which are either inappropriate or wrongly used.

Hydrotherapy at home

Taking a horse to a commercial therapy yard is well out of the reach of many owners, so what use of water can they make in their horses' management and care?

Cold hosing has long been used to counteract heat in horses' legs but it is time consuming as it has to be done three or four times a day to be effective and maintained for about twenty minutes at a time. In all but the warmest weather, it is important to dry off the heels and pastern area after hosing as frequently wet legs *which are not properly dried off afterwards* do develop dry skin and this can lead to chapped skin and maybe infection such as mud fever/scratches even in summer. Blot the legs firmly with old towels (less potentially damaging to possibly weakened skin than rubbing), maybe use a hand-held hairdryer and apply a moisturising or barrier skin lotion to the heels and pasterns which will help. Then to finish off bandage the legs loosely with loose-knit or open weave bandages.

Cold boots and wraps are now available which contain water and are kept in the freezer when not in use: these are very convenient and, if the horse is at livery, can be taken to the yard from home and kept cold by being transported in insulated camping boxes. Again, though, they need to be put on and removed several times a day, really. About twenty minutes a time is adequate. Over-chilling an area can actually kill off tissues. The old favourite of a bag of frozen peas bandaged on over a single layer of muslin or bandage (to prevent over-chilling) is as good as ever.

Whirlpool boots are available plus cold-hosing boots, but horses need to be gradually accustomed to them and, in my experience, not just stood with a haynet and left to get on with it but kept within view in case they become upset or startled and start to play up.

By all means use what natural facilities you can find in your area but check (probably by walking or wading in yourself) what state the bottom is in. Horses may invent their own water games if there are facilities in their field: just make sure, again, that the bottom is safe and also the access. In winter, such facilities may freeze over and constitute a danger so should possibly be fenced off.

Washing horses

Decades ago it was regarded almost as a sin to wash horses because it dried out the skin and removed the natural gloss from the coat. There is certainly something in this argument. Horses which are frequently shampooed have a superficial shine rather than a deep gloss which coat dressings cannot rectify. The coat also does not lie really flat to the skin but has a slightly fluffy feel to it. Part of the problem is using shampoo too often rather than clear water which does a good enough job without the disadvantages provided the horse is walked and dried off properly afterwards. Shampooing should really be reserved for when horses are very dirty or greasy.

From a therapy point of view, water on the body can have a cooling and refreshing effect when horses are hot or working in hot conditions. Water is a good conductor of heat and enables the excess heat to be transferred from the skin to the outside. Sweat performs the same job but cooling a horse by dousing him with *cool* water – not warm or cold – is safe and effective.

The research done for the Atlanta Olympic Games resulted in scotching an old viewpoint, that of not applying water to the loins and hindquarters for fear that the horse would tie up. Muscle mass areas are rich in blood and it is precisely these areas which need to be wetted to enable maximum heat to escape. Cool water, poured, sponged or sprayed on (use a car wash attachment) is beneficial and helps the horse to recover and feel better quicker.

Most stable yards overlook to fit a very simple facility which would enable them to have water of any temperature on tap. It is not practical to keep boiling kettles to add to buckets of cold water which is what most people are faced with who do not want to shock their horses with cold water, so why not have installed an instant water heater fitted to the tap which takes the hosepipe? These heaters are cheap and effective and any plumber or competent DIY enthusiast could fix it up.

MAGNET THERAPY

This therapy is one about which there is still a good deal of disagreement and controversy. Those who have tried the application of magnets to their horses report varying degrees of success but there does not seem to have been much research into the physiology of how magnetism affects the horse, although there is obviously no doubt about the general effects of the world's magnetic field on all life. Just because a technique or therapy has not revealed its 'inner workings' – or has not been proved to work – it does not mean that it has no effect.

Magnetism is believed by many of its proponents to work by improving the efficiency of the blood as regards its ability to carry oxygen and iron in the red substance called haemoglobin. Iron is a metal, of course, so it could be that it is affected by the magnetic force in some way that is beneficial to its use by the body, maybe by increasing the blood's ability to carry both iron and oxygen.

Our bodies are composed of innumerable electrically-charged atoms which hold tissues together and maintain their integrity. Electricity is energy and so the atoms are responsible for the functioning of all the body's biological processes. Presumably, placing a magnet (which itself is electrically charged) on or very close to injured tissue could bring about a change in the atoms and enhance healing.

Yet others feel that the massive amount of man-generated electricity in the world today has an adverse affect on the natural electro-magnetism of the earth based in its rocks and that wearing magnets or undergoing electro-magnetic (pulsed) therapy helps to rebalance our own natural magnetism, to the benefit of health and well-being.

Whatever the case, the jury is still out but some users of magnetism for themselves and their animals swear by it.

There are two main sorts of magnetic therapy on the market – 'ordinary' magnets which rely on their integral electricity to work and magnetism which is electrically pulsed into the body. Some maintain that only the latter can have an effect whereas, of course, others maintain that the non-pulsed type can also be effective. My own experience of magnet therapy is that both types can help and I have never noted any harmful effects from either method.

Non-electrically pulsed magnetism comes in the form of pastern bands, boots, collars and rugs which contain magnets and are normally advised to be left on the horse overnight. The pulsed types need a source of mains electricity and must be used in accordance with the manufacturer's or a therapist's instructions. The pulsed type of magnetism is said to speed up the movement of nutrients and oxygen through the tissues and also the removal of toxins: it does appear to have more of an effect, I feel, than the other type, which can be used alone or to follow up on a treatment with the pulsed type.

Many people wear magnetic bracelets and similar items and there is no physical sensation at all – no tingling, no 'pulling' feeling and certainly nothing like an electric shock! Apparently it works better if the bracelets are not worn all the time but only at night, but some people wear their bracelets or ankle bands all the time. One of my old and arthritic dogs certainly appeared to benefit, as did a similarly-affected pony and my old mare, but a second dog of mine did not seem to be helped at all.

What is magnet therapy used for?

Pulsed magnetic field magnetism is used for recent tissue injuries, any type of osteoarthritic condition such as joint wear and tear, splints and spavins, aches and pains from work or cold or wet weather, general stiffness, physical trauma such as may be sustained during work or an accident in the field and for generally relaxing tense, nervous and highly-sensitive people and animals.

Static field magnetism is used for scrapes and bruises, soft tissue and bone disorders in general, tiredness, stiffness, osteoarthritis and inflammation.

When not to use magnets

- On pregnant mares.
- On blood-filled swellings (haematomas).
- In cases of local infection or systemic infections.
- Directly on inflamed areas.
- Any areas of the body which may contain metal such as a plate on a broken bone or a replacement joint.
- Severe acute injuries.
- On people or animals who are taking cortisone.

From a management viewpoint, a magnetic rug, for instance, could:

- Help an elderly horse who suffered from the cold and wet by enhancing his circulation and perhaps helping to keep him warmer and flexible.
- Help a horse after a journey who arrived at venues tensed up and stiff due to the fact that his muscles have had to constantly work during the trip to help him balance, creating toxins in the muscles which must be eliminated before competing.
- Help horses to warm up quicker before work, if, say, a magnetic rug has been worn overnight or for a few hours beforehand. I feel such horses, who may be older or in hard work, do benefit from wearing such rugs.
- Help horses after work to cool down and expel the toxins created during the muscular activity of work, therefore settling and feeling better quicker.

It is important that magnetic treatment of either kind is not seen as a way of putting off calling in a vet or other professional therapist. I like to think of magnetism as a support therapy for use with others which may be orthodox or complementary. It is always important to get to the root of whatever is causing symptoms and not to skimp on professional help and advice. As a management/home therapy technique and also as a back-up to professional advice and other treatments I feel it is well worth using.

MASSAGE

Massage as we know it today in the west has its roots in ancient eastern, principally Chinese, civilisations. Like many other complementary therapies, it was brought to the west by explorers and travellers and used here, where we had, until very recently, very little knowledge of the eastern philosophy of energy, life force, meridians and the (w)holistic view of health and healing.

Massage, physiotherapy and shiatsu, all covered in this book, have many techniques in common, as illustrated. Here Vick is using careful fingertip pressure on suspect muscles to check for soreness. Theo does not react so she moves on to a different spot

When massage was first applied, it was purely a physical process with scant if any regard for such a mysterious, non-western thing as Life Force and, until fairly recently, that is how matters remained. Now, however, massage therapists appear to be working more along the lines of TCM (Traditional Chinese Medicine) and taking account of energy flow and meridians in addition to specific massage movements and techniques.

Why Massage?

Massage is used for a great deal more than just relaxing a horse and making him feel good after work. A fully trained massage therapist is a very skilled bodyworker but there are simple basic movements and techniques which owners can use on their own horses to not only help them but actually do some good as far as prevention of problems and alleviation of existing ones.

As always, it is best to book a therapist (on veterinary referral in some countries, including the UK) to come and assess your horse, discuss his work and lifestyle and show you simple daily or weekly 'maintenance' techniques to be used in between professional visits. I am very much in favour of any horse, whether it is working or resting, having an appropriate massage now and then (as advisable) from a skilled professional who should also show the owner how to keep up the good work meanwhile.

Reasons to Massage:

- Helping to alleviate soreness, fatigue, tension and minor muscle spasms after work or competition.
- Helping to rid the muscles of waste products such as lactic acid, the result of work. Massage enhances the flow of toxin-laden venous blood so that the waste products are removed sooner and more effectively than might otherwise be the case.
- As an aid to the lymphatic system, which has no pump to move the lymph around the body, to keep the fluid flowing.
- Relaxing the horse according to what kind of massage is used, usually effleurage (see page 112).
- Stimulating the horse, usually by using tapotment or percussion such as clapping or hacking movements.
- Improving the circulation in horses on a restricted, stabled régime such as box rest or when a horse cannot be turned out to move naturally and, especially, roll which is the horse's own version of massage, chiropractic and osteopathy. It is also helpful to increase circulation with massage before significant work such as hunting or a competition to prepare the horse to cope with the demands to be made on his body.
- Preventing adhesions in injured tissues and areas and improving healing.
- Relieving injury, whether acute or chronic.
- Very gentle pressure on inflamed areas, towards the heart generally, can help to disperse congested fluid which has congregated from damaged cells, and the horse will probably also have anti-inflammatory drugs to aid this process.
- Because the skin is the site of many acupuncture/acupressure points and reflex points which affect functioning, manipulating the skin and underlying tissues can help to stimulate them as well as, it is believed, promoting the flow of the body's natural pain-killers, endorphins and encephalins as well as cortisol and so help the horse to feel better during recovery.

When not to massage

- Do not directly massage injured areas but, with advice, apply gentle massage to the surrounding areas to help disperse excess fluid and energy.
- Do not massage animals suffering from systemic disease.
- Do not massage pregnant mares without first taking professional advice.
- Do not continue to massage any area which does not appear to be relieved of spasm, tension or soreness by your efforts. Consult your vet and then your therapist.

Preparing yourself

Massage can be hard work and you have to be fairly strong in the hands, arms, shoulders, back and knees in order to do it effectively and safely. In itself, performing massage will build you up but some preliminary preparation is a good idea.

Your hands need to be flexible and strong and the following will help:

- Increase your hand span by opening your hands and fingers as far as possible and pressing them against a wall, leaning lightly against it, holding for five to ten seconds and then closing your hands into a fist. Repeat a couple of times.
- The grip of the hands can be strengthened by squeezing first a soft rubber ball and then a tennis ball.
- Supple up your wrists by leaning against a wall with your fingers and thumbs spread out and dropping your wrists down carefully, stretching the tissues carefully. Hold for about ten seconds, flex your wrists the other way, then repeat once.
- Fingers can be strengthened by putting a strong elastic band round the ends of all your fingers and opening and closing them; obviously this has an effect on your index and little fingers.
- Do the same thing for your thumb by placing the band around that, too.
- Circle the thumbs both ways several times, clench and unclench your hands and then shake them loose to relax them.

To strengthen your arms and shoulders:

- Do 'press-aways' against a wall. Spread your hands out on a wall at shoulder height and width and, with your elbows slightly bent and standing at arm's length away from the wall, allow yourself to drop (in a controlled way) towards the wall then push yourself slowly back again. Start with five at a time once a day and increase as you improve. Keep your back straight and flat and your knees straight but not stiff.

Your back also needs strength and flexibility but you may wish to check with a physiotherapist or massage therapist before doing back exercises, particularly if you have a weak back or old injury. The author has found the following to be a good exercise to stretch, tone and relax back muscles and relieve them of spasm which is very common.

- Lie on your back on the floor (on a comfortable mat) or a bed with a pillow or cushion under your head, your knees up and feet flat on the floor. Tense the muscles of your abdomen and upper thighs slightly and press the small of your back/spine down to the floor or mattress. Count to five and release. Repeat five times.

111

An exercise to strengthen the back is:

- Lie on your front with your arms down by your sides and carefully lift one (straight) leg at a time up from the floor only an inch or so. Lower it and lift the other leg. As you become stronger in the back, this exercise can be done with your arms stretched up and out beside your ears and the arms, and your head, can also be lifted. Do not push this exercise. A slight movement is all that is necessary (or usually possible) to improve the strength in the relevant muscles.

Checking for problems

As with other bodywork therapies, it is usual to assess the horse visually and also by means of stroking movements and others over his body. A professional therapist will only work on a horse after a veterinary referral and should have diagnosis from the vet, if there is a known, specific problem, so will have an idea what to look for but may well come up with something else, maybe related but not obvious. There may be no particular problem, the owner simply wanting the horse to have the benefits of an assessment and professional massage.

A full, professional assessment can take a good half hour or longer. The horse is looked at from a distance and will be walked and maybe trotted up for the therapist, turned in circles, backed, maybe moved sideways according to what he or she asks for. The therapist may want to watch the horse in his box, in the field, on the lunge or long reins and under saddle. Therapists are often very good at assessing how much damage, if any, the rider is doing to the horse - not to mention the saddle, bridle, bit and training aids!

He or she will then palpate or feel the horse to detect areas which may result in a pain or other adverse response from the horse. He may move away, snap or bite, put his ears back, swish his tail or stamp, so do watch him carefully during this process. Even just a discomfited facial expression is a good sign that he is uncomfortable being palpated or moved in a particular part of his body.

You can give your horse an all-over assessment yourself with the stroking technique. Using the flat of your hand, stroke firmly but gently and slowly all over the horse with the lie of the hair, starting behind the ears and logically moving all over the body backwards and downwards as when grooming. Feel for any unusually warm areas which may indicate injury or cold ones which may mean poor circulation, uneven tone, lumps or hard areas which may indicate spasm. It takes experience to detect these but an owner with feel actually has an advantage over a therapist who does not know the horse as she will do this or something like it when grooming just about every day and will have a running mental record of the horse's condition.

Techniques

Massage is a skilled therapy and not all the techniques are suitable for untrained owners to apply. It is helpful to understand the techniques a professional might apply, however. Bony areas are avoided in massage including the ribs and abdomen (these areas should also not be groomed heavily either) and also the throat.

Effleurage

This is a basic and very useful technique for a general all-over massage. It is basically stroking in a specific way. Place your hand or hands flat but relaxed, so that they mould to the tissues beneath them, on the horse and work with the direction of the hair. Work down the top and sides of the neck, down the chest between the forelegs, down the front of the shoulder blade,

Pauline demonstrates the effleurage technique on Rose who is being restrained by Janet from eating the holly trees to her left!

around the back of the shoulder blade and elbow and under the girth area, along the sides of the back and quarters to the tail, down towards the stifle, down the sides of the thighs and in around the muscles between the hindlegs. The legs themselves are massaged upwards against the lie of the hair as this helps disperse any 'stagnant' fluid or energy there.

To perform effleurage:
Use the same flat but soft and moulding posture of the hands and you can use one hand or both. Start on the areas away from the central body mass such as the top of the neck, back and quarters or on the legs, and work towards the centre of the body. Place your hands on your chosen area with your arms firm but not stiff and slightly bent at the elbows. Lean your weight on to your hands and push your hands along, away from yourself. Straighten up and, keeping the hands on the horse, reduce the pressure to just a touch as you bring them back, then repeat for your next stroke.

In horses not used to this or to any grooming such as correct, traditional body brushing, which involves pressure, use a light pressure at first, increasing it for more benefit as the horse becomes used to it.

On the legs, use your palms and the heels of your hands with your fingers moulding round the legs and work upwards carefully.

This type of massage 'grounds' and relaxes your horse mentally and physically gets the circulation of blood, lymph and energy moving.

Petrissage, compression or wringing:
This technique aids the flow of blood and lymph, also energy so helping to remove toxins. It can help to restore and increase the mobility of tissues and promote their strength and integrity and may implement skin reflexes and those of the underlying tissues for enhanced functioning.

The therapist will apply compression by gently grasping the tissues under the skin between the fingers, palms and heels of the hand, 'pick up' the tissues, squeeze them gently and release the pressure so that the tissue returns to its normal position. This is carried out on the upper legs.

Compressions involving pressure from the heel of the hand, palms and fingers apply sideways, twisting movement of the hand and then release of the pressure; this is effective on muscle mass areas. The skin is moved on the underlying tissue and the hand is slid across to the next area.

Wringing is often used on the crest of the neck. The hands are draped across the mane line and one hand draws the tissues towards the therapist whilst the other pushes them away. Work all the way down the neck like this to relax your horse and his neck tissues.

Kneading:
In this technique a fist is formed and the knuckles and the middle bones of the fingers press down into the muscle, twist slightly towards the thumb and then lift up again. Kneading reaches deeper tissues and may be done with some force by a trained therapist.

Percussion or tapotment:
This is very stimulating of energy and the horse's attitude. You can use loose fists, bouncing them alternately up and down on the sides of the hands in a loose but firm tapping movement, using mainly the movement of the wrists and forearms. Like wisping, the result should be 'flinching' (contraction) of the muscles and also relaxation in time with the taps. This is used on muscle mass areas.

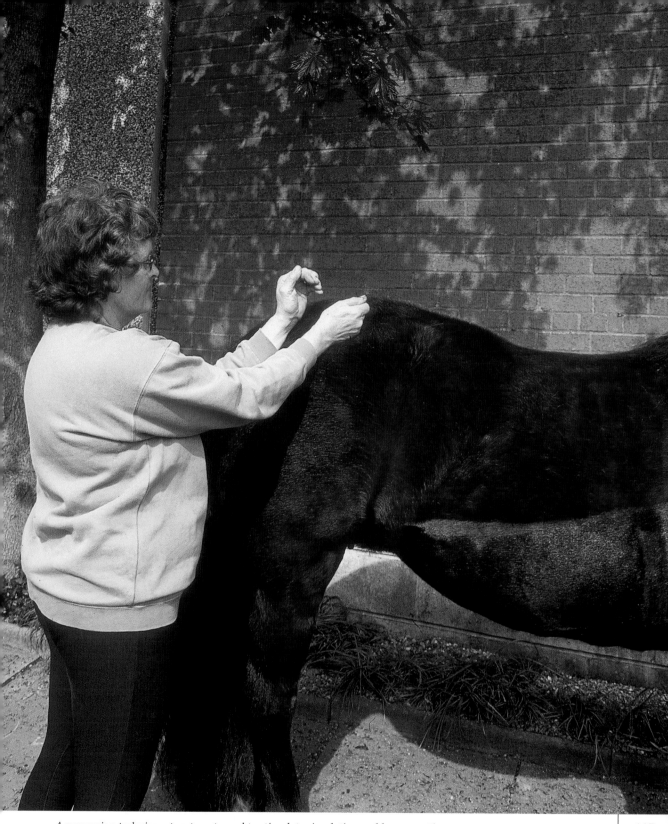

A percussion technique, tapotment, used to stimulate circulation and loosen up tissues

OPPOSITE: *Another percussion technique – clapping with cupped hands. Some horses unused to bodywork other than grooming can be a little alarmed by these techniques, so go very gently at first*

Clapping:
The hands are cupped with the bottom knuckles uppermost in a roof shape. The hand remains fairly relaxed and the movement is from the wrist. Each hand alternately moves up and down on to the muscle area so that the fingertips and the heels of the hand only make contact. Clapping is clearly stimulating and moves blood, lymph and energy along.

Hacking:
This is another stimulating technique done with the little finger sides of relaxed hands, again moving up and down from the wrists alternately over muscle areas smaller than the main masses.

Friction:
Friction is used across the lie of the muscle areas in small areas such as spasm or where adhesions are known to exist. The middle finger is placed over the index finger for added support and stability and the area worked across the fibre direction, back and forth, moving the skin with it, often in a small oval movement. The word friction does not mean that the skin is rubbed but that the skin remains in place under the finger and the underlying tissues are subjected to friction. It is very effective at loosening up painful 'knots' in the muscles.

DIY Techniques

The techniques which should be suitable for owners to apply are effleurage, wringing on the neck, percussion, hacking and clapping.

You could start a session by all-over stroking and progress to effleurage to get things moving and settle the horse. Then apply wringing to the neck which, again, loosens up the neck and relaxes the horse mentally. Stimulate the circulation and loosen up the muscles with any of the other three techniques and finish off with effleurage again and finally stroking. As with grooming, always work in the same order so that no part is overlooked. I always work the left side first from front to back, then the right side. If you want to stimulate your horse before work, finish with a stimulating technique such as a little more hacking or clapping, not stroking.

This sort of routine *will* be effective and the horse will come to know your movements and be quite content to stand and co-operate or eat his hay as you work.

If your therapist thinks at any time that the other techniques are needed, he or she may show you precisely how to do them or may feel that you should confine your efforts to those five mentioned.

Massage is often combined with stretching and the application of aromatherapy oils so be prepared to alter your routine according to what is needed.

You will find massage hard work at first and some equine sports massage therapists have very muscular arms and shoulders to prove it! The work will benefit you, too, in a different way, but it is yet another bodywork technique you can add to your repertoire to help your horse and build on your relationship.

ABOVE: *Lucy is an elderly mare who benefits from careful stretches. Janet is standing with a fairly wide base of support with her feet although the left leg could be further back for increased stability. She supports Lucy's leg under the fetlock and knee for increased comfort.*

BELOW: *Lucy tends to stand a little splay footed, so Janet supports her leg on her thigh and performs inward rotations of the hoof to help to counteract this stance*

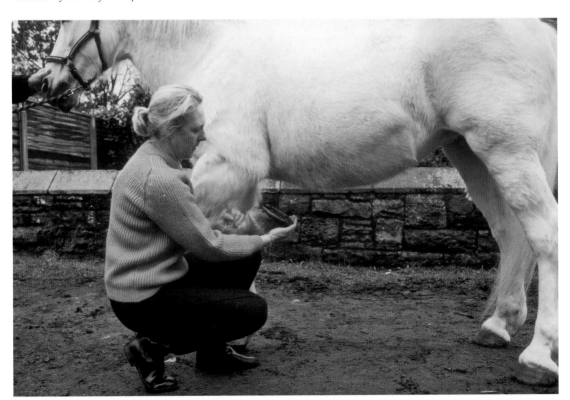

Vick uses the heel of her hand to gently apply massaging pressure to Theo's shoulder muscles

PHYSIOTHERAPY

As most readers will know, physiotherapy is not a single therapy but a collective name for several or indeed many physical therapies, mainly involving the use of electrically operated machines. That aspect of it is outside the intended scope of this book which is meant to detail simple methods of management and therapeutic techniques which involve little if any financial outlay and no specialist equipment but mainly the use of the horse owner's own two hands plus, on occasion, the use of ordinary tack and equipment which can be found in any stable yard or home.

Physiotherapists are highly skilled therapists who are now regularly accepted by the more forward-thinking veterinary practices: vets now often suggest a referral to a physiotherapist for certain injuries and conditions.

The purposes of physiotherapy are to not only assist in quicker and more effective healing of injured tissues but also in health and physical maintenance. Some of the therapies mentioned in this book may be included in a physiotherapist's armoury, for example massage, stretches, magnet therapy and hydrotherapy. A good physiotherapist will be trained to expertly assess a horse standing still in his box and behaving as he normally does, led in hand at walk and trot, lunged in canter, asked to perform various movements such as circles, backing and lateral work in hand, going free in his field and under saddle. The therapist needs to be able to work out why a horse is moving in a particular way and will understand that the cause of an apparent problem in one part of the horse's body may well be caused by pain in a different part. She, or he, will need to be able to study and assess muscular development (is it even or not from side to side?), the conformation of the horse (which could be unsuited to the job he has been given), the way the legs move (normal or crooked?), the balance of the feet (which are the basis of everything) and many more factors. She will examine the horse by touch as well, noting any differences in tone and texture of skin and underlying tissues, any areas of soreness, tension or pain, spasm, heat and cold.

At the end of all this, she should be able to give you her opinion in relation to the veterinary diagnosis. She may arrive in your yard a few days later than the vet's original visit and things could have changed for better or worse and because she is trained just as highly in her specialised field as a vet is in his or her more general one, her current findings should be noted and possibly discussed with your vet. The vet and therapist should work together and should certainly bring the owner into their discussions (which I am afraid does not always happen) so that he or she is kept fully in the picture about just what is wrong with the horse, what treatment the therapist is going to give and what follow-up treatment the owner can and/or needs to give between visits.

Obviously, the use of machines is the field of the therapist but such matters as hot and cold applications, controlled walking in hand, box or groundwork exercises, administration of any medicines, integration with other therapies such as herbal or homoeopathic remedies, shiatsu or specialised nutritional supplements concern the owner.

What is physiotherapy used for?

The following are the main uses of physiotherapy. Not all may be required in the care of a particular horse, of course.

Therapists sometimes check a horse's ability to raise his back by pressing reflex points on either side of the root of the tail, usually with the thumbs. Theo's back came up immediately – no problem there

- To enhance the healing of injured tissues.
- To relieve pain and discomfort in the horse.
- To help reduce the formation of scar tissue and adhesions during healing.
- To promote cellular function and activity which is the basis of healing; this produces heat (required after the initial period of inflammation has subsided) which promotes healing.
- To cause rhythmic muscular effort or contraction which promotes fluid drainage from an injured area, improving circulation of blood, lymph and energy which will help to prevent the deterioration arising from loss of use.

Cold therapy

The initial period of possibly intense inflammation of an injury such as an injured tendon, ligament or muscle by tearing, abrasion or bruising, could last about forty-eight hours. The body mobilises its defences and things should be starting to subside noticeably by that time. Anti-inflammatory drugs will probably have been administered, maybe, depending on the injury and the site, supportive, comfortable bandages will have been applied to an injured leg and also to its opposite number which will be taking more weight, and the horse should be feeling more comfortable.

It may be advised that the owner applies cold packs to the area and this may be by means of hosing, special boots in which the horse stands, or by strapping or bandaging on crushed ice (or the formerly popular and effective frozen peas) in a cold-pad or ice-pack several times a day. Cold compresses made by dipping towels or other fabric in iced water may also be recommended although the old way of bandaging them on and leaving them is rather pointless as the body temperature will soon heat up the fabric. The owner or handler may need to apply gentle massage with, say, a plain ice 'lolly' on a stick or a bag of crushed ice or ice cubes and supplies of ice must be available all the time for this.

Cold therapy is used for *recent* soft tissue injury and works by helping to prevent excessive swelling and congestion of an area. Ice should therefore be taken in the transport vehicle in an insulated travelling box to competitions or 'away-days' as, by the time you return home severe inflammation may well have occurred.

The massage technique with ice is to use gentle circular movements for about fifteen to twenty minutes, after which you should notice a difference in the tissues. On the leg, such as down the tendons or around the ligaments, use the 'lolly' in an up and down movement. Rest the area for twenty to thirty minutes and then repeat the ice massage for another fifteen to twenty minutes.

How does cold therapy work?
The application of cold to an area causes constriction or narrowing of the superficial blood vessels which is a natural response by the body. The body wishes to maintain its normal, comfortable temperature, most particularly deep inside it so that vital organs are protected. Therefore, the superficial blood vessels narrow to send the blood deeper into the body. Swelling is reduced and more fluid cannot get into the area. This helps to control bleeding and swelling. The cells in the area 'go slow' so that little oxygen is needed.

OPPOSITE: *Probably the technique owners are most likely to be asked to carry out is the application of cold. In this photograph, Pauline is massaging Rose's shoulder muscles in circular movements with a bag of frozen peas – always a good old standby. They can also be bandaged on the legs over a layer of gauze*

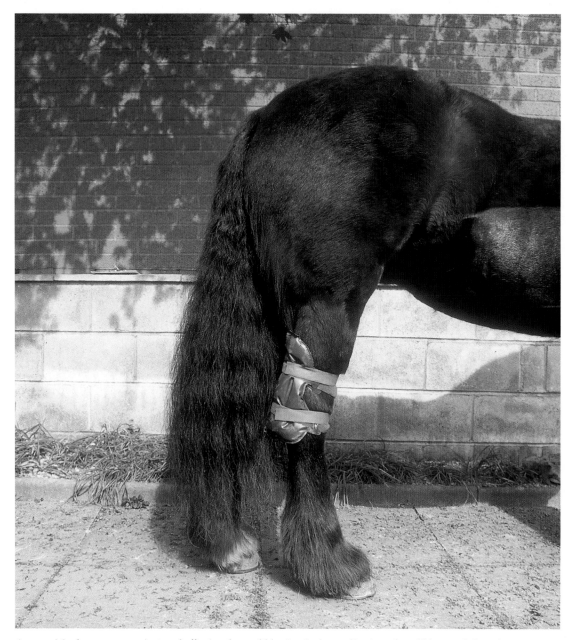

ABOVE: *Much more convenient and effective than cold hosing is the application of a cold boot to help reduce inflammation and swelling. Comprising water-filled pockets, these boots are kept in the freezer ready for use at any time. They are available in various designs for different parts of the legs*

OPPOSITE: *A good hold for massaging the horse's legs (upwards to help to disperse fluid) is to link the fingers and either roll the heels of the hands in an upward motion or bring the clasped hands up the leg together, applying gentle to moderate pressure depending on whether or not the leg is tender*

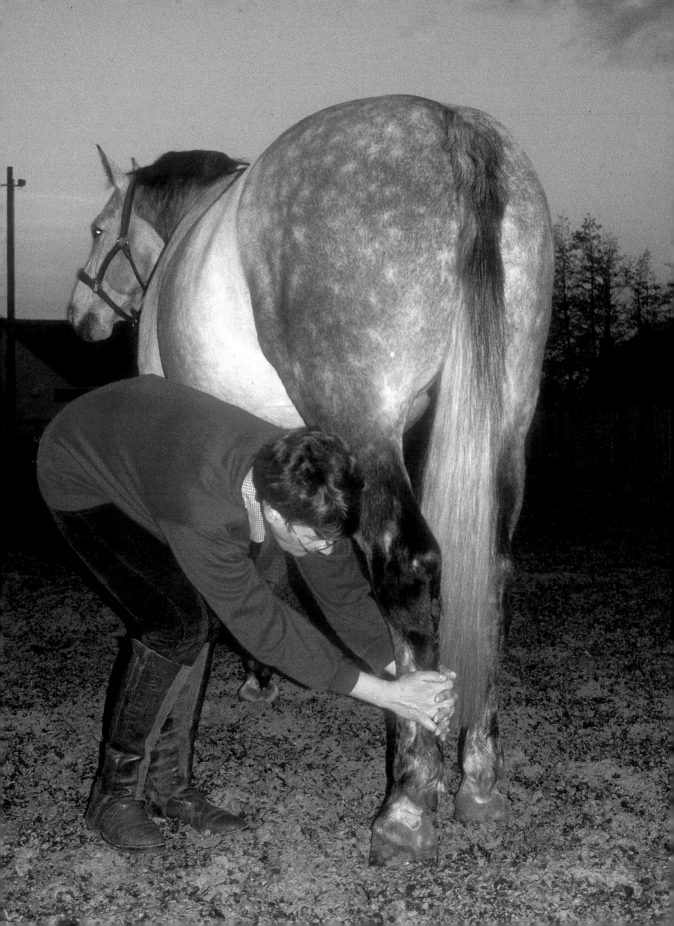

After twenty minutes' application (although some therapists say less), deeper vessels dilate/expand as the heat and cold sensors and regulators in the body sense that the area is too cold for safety and needs warming up, bringing fresh blood to the area. However, a second application repeats the process. There is also a slight pain-reducing effect and lessening of tension with the cold application.

Depending on your advice, you may be asked to apply cold every two or three hours, either by means of ice or very cold water. The combination of gentle compression by either massage or the pressure of the water, plus subsequent relaxation of the tissues reduces the heat by cooling the area and improving the circulation in and around it.

Excess cold and freezing can certainly damage and kill off tissues so cold applications must not be sustained beyond the recommended time. Also, such applications will not be recommended in cases where there is significant nerve damage or reduced blood circulation.

Heat therapy

This may be recommended after the initial days of cold application are over and the heat and inflammation have reduced. Heat can be applied by the owner using packs heated by microwave, water heated to the temperature advised by the therapist, by means of hot compresses, and may be alternated with cold applications to achieve alternate vasodilation and vasoconstriction (expansion and narrowing of the blood vessels) respectively. This is felt to improve circulation and affect the deeper circulation as well, all aimed at bringing blood and healing substances (oxygen and nutrients) to the injured area. Heat can be applied by the therapist using specialised machines. There is a school of thought that keeping a horse warm prior to work makes the soft tissues more pliable and less prone to injury. Certainly, cold causes muscles to contract and 'stiffen' up which is never good for work.

The effects of superficial heat application help to reduce pain and stiffness, enhance metabolic activity in the tissues and generally make the horse feel good provided it is not excessive. The use of heated boxes, heat retaining rugs and bandages, solarium sessions and the like are generally good for horses, comforting and healing if used with discretion and under appropriate advice. It helps to keep sick or distressed horses warm, helps to warm up and dry off wet horses particularly those who have swum when they are often very cold (as most pools are not heated and the energy output is insufficient to keep the horse warm in cold water, I believe) and has health enhancing benefits generally. Full-spectrum lights and heat lamps are not that expensive and can usefully be fitted to any loose box for their benefits.

Other physiotherapy techniques such as long-reining, in-hand leading and horse walkers have been dealt with in this book and several excellent books are available on physiotherapy written at a level most owners can understand. A good therapist forms part of a working horse's team with the vet, farrier, nutritionist and teacher.

SHIATSU

Shiatsu is a Japanese, holistic system of healing and health maintenance based on principles used in humans and animals for over 5000 years. It is closely related to acupuncture and acupressure and works on the same principles but does not employ needles. It works mainly on the energy meridians or channels by means of static pressure (i.e. not rubbing or massaging) to influence energy flow and encourage balance to be maintained or restored. Some elements of shiatsu, though, use exercises, stretches and massage-type movements.

It may sound like a bodywork system which is hard for owners to understand and use themselves on their own horses but, in practice, its basic principles, to a useful level, can be learned from short courses and books which are available. It is far preferable to attend a course under a qualified and sensitive practitioner (try to get a word-of-mouth recommendation here) than to only use a book, however, because it is important to absorb the spirit and feel of the therapy under expert tuition and supervision.

The prominence of shiatsu in the United Kingdom is largely due to the efforts of my own trainer, the late Pamela Hannay, who was Senior Instructor of the Ohashi Institute in New York and Europe where she also served on the Board of Directors. She trained extensively in Japan and began teaching and practising shiatsu in 1978. Then in 1983 an opportunity arose for her to treat a badly injured horse which enabled her subsequently to translate and develop shiatsu principles for working with horses.

The opinion of some therapists, in this and other methods, is that in the east training in oriental medicine can take many years and it cannot be learned by reading a book or attending a short course. This was not the view of Pamela who firmly believed, and demonstrated time and again, that a genuinely interested, sensitive, reasonably intelligent person can obtain a useful working knowledge and learn the basic principles of shiatsu to a level which would enable them to benefit horses, their own or, later, other people's. Further training was and is available for those who would like to work professionally. The major book she wrote is included in the Reading List. Owners who want to help their own horses are well advised, in my view, to engage a professional practitioner, as detailed above, most of whom should be happy to teach and develop their effectiveness.

What happens during a shiatsu session?

The word 'shiatsu' means 'finger pressure'. Practitioners use mainly their fingers, hands and arms to exert specialised pressures, stretches and rotations on the body to encourage or modify the flow of the body's 'life force', energy or 'qi' (pronounced 'kee'). There is no compulsion involved in shiatsu and nothing uncomfortable or distressing. In fact, horses, being such tactile and sensitive animals, enjoy it and respond well. Practitioners work with their hands in a gentle, safe and natural way with muscles, tendons and ligaments, but also with energy flow to balance it and help the body or mind to heal itself naturally, or simply to help maintain existing good health and prevent disorders. After a session, not only specific relief and improvement may be noticed but also a general feeling of increased suppleness, overall relaxation, revitalisation and well-being.

The basis of shiatsu

If the body's energy flow is not unimpeded and free, health problems can arise, it is believed, in both body and mind. Shiatsu is gentle, non-invasive and can be relaxing or stimulating, according to need. It is used for health maintenance as well as disease and disorder and for treating physical, emotional and psychological problems. Your horse does not need to have a 'problem' to benefit from shiatsu: it is excellent for a periodic, beneficial treat for everything from working athletes to pony pals. For a general, professional pampering to enhance your horse's suppleness, well-being and feel-good mood, there is, in my view, simply nothing like it.

Several eastern civilisations believe that the body has an energy force which flows around the body in meridians or channels beneath the skin and sometimes deeper within the body, passing right round the body within one day-night cycle. Pressure of varying kinds along these different meridians can speed up, slow down or free the flow of qi upon which mental and physical health depends. After a full shiatsu session, it is advised that the patient rests for, ideally, twenty-four hours to allow the qi to respond to the treatment.

Many of the meridians are named after body organs (bladder, liver, stomach etc.) although they may not be centred around that organ. It is believed that stimulation of those meridians enhances not only the condition of the areas of the body through which they run but also fulfils the same purpose for the organs after which they are named. For example, working the bladder meridian, one of the key meridians, encourages the excretion of toxins and other wastes from the body. The kidney meridian is also worked after the bladder meridian as the two complement each other's functions. Other meridians have different purposes.

Along the meridians (and at other sites) are points which are used in acupuncture (where needles are inserted) and acupressure (where finger or thumb pressure, normally, is used). These points can be used in shiatsu but can wait until you have more experience and knowledge. They are points where the energy is believed to flow particularly close to the surface and where stimulation affects particular organs and parts of the body. Acupressure

The red line indicates the routes of the bladder meridian and the green line its complementary kidney meridian. Obviously, the meridians occur on both sides of the body. These are the two 'multi-purpose' meridians which can help any condition so are useful for owners to learn. The bladder meridian (red) runs from front to back on the horse and the kidney meridian (green) from back to front

(which preceded acupuncture as a therapy) gives very many points which you do not need to know unless you wish to train further.

Another concept discussed earlier in the book is that of yin and yang. It may sound like sacrilege to some, but to work effectively at a basic level on your own horse it is not essential to understand this although it is extremely helpful, particularly if you want to become more attuned to shiatsu or eastern therapies and systems in general. Giving a general shiatsu session for all-over well-being, with the intention of goodwill, does, believe it or not, produce good results!

In every energetic quality there is a little of its opposite. They flow together and need each other and represent the duality of every aspect of nature – up and down, sun and shade, loud and quiet and so on. From the point of view of therapy, the eastern concept is that yin is taken to be female, quiet, submissive, receptive and sensitive while yang is male, strong, outgoing and active.

Qi can have different qualities, too, which an experienced practitioner can sense. The words kyo and jitsu describe energy distortions or imbalances along the meridians. Lack of energy, softness, coldness or weakness is described as kyo and excessive energy, fullness, heat or hardness as jitsu. Kyo can relate to yin and jitsu to yang. If energy is depleted in one part (kyo), a blockage or 'traffic jam' (jitsu) results elsewhere. When feeling your horse, along the meridians or otherwise, jitsu is easier to feel than kyo: put rather crudely jitsu can be envisaged as lumps or protrusions and kyo as depressions or hollows. The kyo condition has to be corrected before the jitsu can be dealt with and this is usually just by gentle, sustained 'holding' with the hand, using gentle palm pressure, to allow energy to be drawn from elsewhere in the body – normally the jitsu areas – and arrive where it is needed. This is called 'tonifying'. Jitsu can be influenced by 'sedation', conversely: this may involve pressure of shorter duration or percussive techniques (see below) in the opposite direction to the energy flow of the meridian concerned.

I do realise, because I have been there, that all this sounds strange or difficult for western minds to understand or accept at first, but if you sincerely wish to understand this concept (intent) you will find that it does come to you and, as the medium for the energy, you will have an effect. Reading and further study will be interesting and rewarding.

Do the meridians exist?

This question has been addressed earlier in this book, when I expressed my feeling that the meridians do exist in the form of directions like wind flow or water currents rather than physical, anatomical structures. I have, therefore, never found this difference of opinion over meridians to be a block. Energy is intangible but no one denies that it exists. In some meridians the energy flows upwards and forwards towards the head and in others towards the tail or the ground. (The two most useful meridians for owners to use are detailed below.) Some practitioners say that they can actually feel the energy running beneath their fingers. Sometimes you can see little ripples of muscles which some take to be this energy. I feel that this is normal muscle movement and not specifically the 'life force' type of energy.

I am one of those practitioners who works by intuition as to exactly where the meridians are based on their well-documented positions. However, many orthodox western doctors and health care professionals, despite being faced with the efficacy of acupuncture, shiatsu's sister therapy, are understandably sceptical of working with meridians which have never, so far as I know, been proved to exist anatomically.

Uses of shiatsu

Shiatsu, being both a healing and health maintenance modality, is used for:

- Early recognition and treatment of problems before they build up.
- Improvement of behavioural, temperamental and attitude problems.
- Treatment and elimination of musculo-skeletal problems including chronic and slight lameness and stiffness, and short or incorrect gaits.
- Helping to achieve and maintain suppleness, health and well-being and restoring poor health and condition.
- Reducing susceptibility to injury and disease.
- Maximising physical abilities and potential.
- Stimulating and strengthening the immune system.
- Enhancing the circulation of blood and lymph, the performance of the nervous and endocrine systems and so encouraging the production of the body's own natural painkillers and 'feel-good' hormones and chemicals.
- Promoting a closer and more understanding relationship between horse and owner.

Management and shiatsu

There are many reasons why a horse or pony may be out of sorts, not all of them directly caused by the horse's owner or carers. Something as basic but uncontrollable as the weather can affect some horses, also environmental pollution of various kinds. Other causes are management-related such as poor nutrition, sub-standard stabling and bedding, and lack of liberty, company and an appropriate lifestyle for the individual. Add these to unrecognised pain or stiffness, demanding work, stress, infection, toxins in the environment or feed and an unreliable routine and it becomes understandable that sensitive animals like horses are so often under par and off work. Anything noticeably stressful such as travelling, the absence of a companion, the presence of the vet or farrier or an 'enemy' horse can certainly upset a horse but other more subtle factors which we may not recognise may unbalance the energy flow and could account for the horse, and his performance, being below par.

Manipulations

As well as applying pressure to the meridians to stabilise the flow of qi, there are various gentle movements, rotations and stretches applied to the horse which, in themselves, are designed to have an effect on not only meridians but also the body's soft tissues, joints and some nerves which facilitates not only muscle function but also hormonal release which can have a beneficial effect on both the body and the mind.

In shiatsu, the stretches are not held for more than a very few seconds and neither they nor the rotations are forced. It is a basic tenet of shiatsu that if a horse objects to any part of the treatment three times the practitioner stops attempting that particular movement and goes on to something else. Very often, after a few minutes experiencing some other technique, the horse will allow the movement which previously concerned him.

How often?

As a health maintenance modality, a horse would benefit from a full shiatsu treatment (approximately an hour in length) according to his individual needs and propensities once a week. Much shorter periods of moves and techniques can be applied before and after every ride if the owner wishes, to prepare the horse for work and to encourage the elimination of toxins such as carbon dioxide and lactic acid after work. Horses with health problems would benefit from shiatsu more often than once a week.

In the case of shiatsu, it is advisable to call in a trained practitioner every few months for a 'check-up' treatment. A performance horse in full work would benefit from a professional treatment every month but there is much the owner can do to help the horse on a daily or weekly basis.

Working on your horse

Preparation
The best time for a shiatsu session is when your horse is normally relaxing but not actually dozing or sleeping. You know your and his routines so choose accordingly. If he lives on a busy yard, pick the quietest time possible as loud people, loud noises and a shallow, superficial atmosphere around you definitely detracts from the beneficial potential of shiatsu.

Prepare yourself by calming your mind and doing a little slow deep breathing. Think about and to your horse with shiatsu, relaxation, healing and maybe stimulation in your mind. Do not become at all anxious about what you are going to do. Make your shoulders relaxed, back and down. Centre your awareness down in the centre of your body, or *hara*, just below your navel and think and work from here. This principle can be used, with advantage, when riding, too.

Your nails need to be short for shiatsu as you use your finger ends to press directly down (not at an angle) on the meridians. Remove your watch, rings and earrings for safety, and make sure that you are wearing comfortable clothing but strong, safe boots or shoes. Some people like to wear a hard hat and maybe a body protector but I find these really distracting and, of course, uncomfortable. If the weather is cold, keep your horse partly covered as you work if he normally wears rugs.

Welcome
Even though you know your horse well, it is etiquette to pause at his door and let him sniff and acknowledge you for a few moments. Enter his box and squat down in a corner, or stand quietly if he is fairly new to you, and wait for him to come to you. Have your intent to give him a shiatsu session in your mind. This waiting gives him time to give you permission to treat him. Breathe calmly and try to co-ordinate your breathing with his for a while. Shortly, he will come over and lower his head to you, acknowledging your presence and intentions. Let him sniff you and nuzzle you if he wants to. You can take all this as evidence that he is agreeable and you may start.

Stroking
I always begin on the left side and then do the right side. As the session goes on and I am performing specific moves, I know that I work left to right so nothing is forgotten. You will not wish to do all the moves every day, but you should certainly always begin and end with *all-over stroking*. This 'opens up' or alerts the meridians, it is believed, and readies the energy flow and your horse himself for what is to come. It gently stimulates the skin and structures immediately beneath and makes the horse very aware of his body. Stroking is either very relaxing if done

131

OPPOSISTE: *Always begin and end a shiatsu session with all-over stroking in a hand-over-hand motion, leaving each hand on the horse until the other has made contact so that you are always in touch with the energy*

slowly and lightly (but not so light as to tickle the horse which is very irritating) but more stimulating if done faster and with a firmer pressure. It gives you the chance to sense any areas which may need attention – tightness, soreness or heat (jitsu) or cold, trembling and flaccid (kyo).

Stand a little away from your horse and work from your centre, leaning gently into the horse, and begin. Always, during meridian work, keep one hand (your supporting or control hand) on the horse at all times to keep the energy connection. The other hand is your working hand. Have your feet about hip width apart and the leg behind your working hand slightly behind the other, for balance and security of stance. For the stroking, use alternate hands to smooth over the horse *always having at least one hand on the horse*, lifting and stroking with a left, right, left, right motion, always putting one hand on before finishing the stroke and lifting up the other.

The shoulder is a good place to start, particularly if your horse is a bit head-shy. You can go up to the neck area afterwards but do not, early in the session, try to touch the head if the horse does not like this.

When you have stroked one side, keep one hand on the horse and walk round him to begin the other side and repeat. Stroke with the lie of the hair and all the way down the legs. To finish the stroking, gently encircle the dock with your hands and run them down it, lifting it very slightly to check its condition and the horse's reaction.

Do not chat to the horse which will distract you both, but now and then say a brief word or two and all the time watch him for his reaction, also noting whether or not he moves away from you in general or when any particular area is reached.

Meridian work

The two *meridians* which owners can and should work on (and at this introductory stage you do not need to know any more meridians) are the bladder and kidney meridians (see page 128). The bladder meridian is a key meridian in that it regulates the flow of energy in all the meridians and is believed to assist the functions of the bladder. The kidney meridian complements it and is believed to govern all body fluids and to help detoxify and 'cleanse' or purify the blood. These functions of both meridians have far-reaching, beneficial effects on the whole body which is why they are basic and important to start with.

The beauty of shiatsu, in my view, is that you do not need, in the early stages, to know about the acupoints but can have an effect just by using the meridians. Also, you do not need to work by pressure the whole of a meridian if the horse is touchy about a particular area or has an injury. Just working as much of the meridian as you can will balance the energy flow sufficiently to help the horse.

If there is an injury on or around the meridian, do not apply pressure but *very* lightly just hold and move your hand over and around it, not even necessarily touching it, and give out healing from your working hand, particularly along the line of the meridian.

The technique of *palming* is used before fingertip pressure. This helps prepare the body and the meridians and gives you the reassurance of not needing to know the precise line of the meridians, especially as a beginner, but will give you a chance to feel where you think the meridians are and to follow your intuition.

OPPOSITE: I prefer to do the meridian work before other movements. Here Vick is palming Theo's bladder meridian, one hand (her left) as the control hand and the other as the working hand.

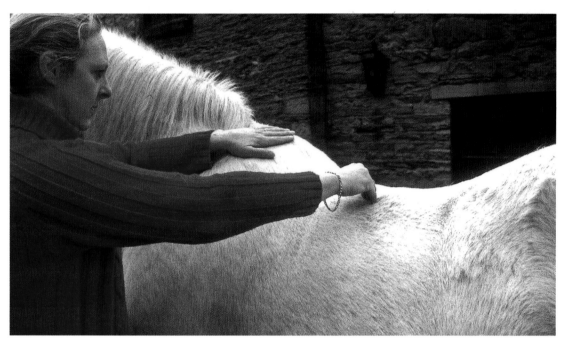

After palming the meridians, work them again using fingertip pressure, as Janet is doing here with Lucy's bladder meridian …

… and here with her kidney meridian

 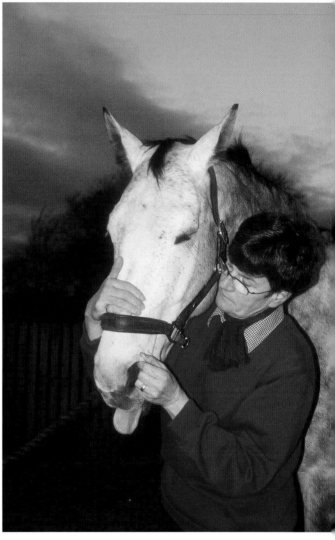

Head and Neck

OPPOSITE: *Rocking the neck gives a good indication of how loose and relaxed the neck is and also helps to loosen it up and relax the horse. If you push the crest of the neck away from yourself and back towards yourself in a rhythmic movement, the muzzle should swing in the opposite direction, i.e. if the crest is pushed away from you the muzzle should swing towards you and vice versa, otherwise there is a problem which may be pain, tension or stiffness or simply lack of relaxation*

ABOVE LEFT: *Light pressure all around the edges of the bones of the eye socket is very relaxing for most horses and works several acupressure points. There are several shiatsu techniques for the head and mouth which help improve the behaviour of headshy horses and those who bite and nip or are forever chewing things*

ABOVE RIGHT: *Gently pinching all around the nostrils with your fingers and thumb activates several acupressure points and greatly improves the attitude of headshy horses*

Stand on the left side of your horse and allow your left (supporting) hand to drape lightly across the withers evenly over the spine. Place your right (working) hand a few inches/centimetres to the side of it (your palm will be on the bladder meridian) and allow your supporting hand to sink into the horse, then allow the working hand to sink in. Feel your horse inside your body and stay for a few seconds. Gradually release the pressure in both hands until the supporting hand has released slightly and the working hand more so, just touching as it slides a few more inches or the width of your hand down the back. Keep your supporting hand where it is and sink in with your working hand and proceed like this to about the loins, at which point you will wish to slide your supporting hand down closer to your working hand, for comfort and connection. Continue like this to the root of the tail.

The supporting hand may help to distract the horse's attention from your working hand if you reach a sensitive area. If you do, lighten your pressure with your working hand, particularly when you are using the fingertip technique, stay for a few seconds (you will know how long) and send in healing, then pass on to the next area along the meridian. All the time you have to concentrate on and mentally and spiritually feel your horse.

When you reach the root of the tail, keep one hand on your horse and walk round to the right side to palm that. Your right hand will now be your supporting hand and your left hand your working hand.

The fingertip technique:
Again, stand a little away from your horse, say on the left hand side, and, working the bladder meridian first, place your right (control) hand gently just over his neck behind the poll. Form a straight, even line with the fingertips of your left hand and press them lightly, but not so lightly that it irritates the horse, on his face up the meridian at its start.

To judge the pressure, use the gauge of nought being no pressure at all and ten being as hard as you could press (which you will never use). Your intuition will, in time, help you to judge the pressure but initially aim for about three, particularly on the head and legs and on horses unused to shiatsu. Press for about one or two seconds (you will come to know when to stay longer), lift and move up to the next part and so on. When you reach the poll, move your supporting hand down to the withers and continue pressing down the bladder meridian, leaning into the horse from your centre with the leg on the side of your working hand slightly behind the other. As you reach the withers with your working hand, make it your supporting hand and work with your right hand all the way down the meridian, if all of it is acceptable to the horse.

You will see from the drawing that there is a second part to the bladder meridian, so when you have reached the foot, keep a hand on the horse and come to the start of the second part of the meridian and repeat the procedure until you reach the spot where they join. I like to place my palm on this point then for a few seconds to finish off the left side.

Then, keeping a hand on your horse, walk round to the right side and repeat the whole procedure. Do not rush and do not poke! *Intend* to help relax and heal your horse – and yourself! When the bladder meridians have been worked, you can palm them again if you have time and see if you can detect any changes in kyo, jitsu or general tension.

Next work the kidney meridian in exactly the same way, palming and fingertip pressure. This, you will note, runs from back to front of the horse unlike the bladder meridian which runs from front to back.

Always be aware of safety. When doing the lower areas, squat or bend your knees, never kneel on the ground. Keep your back flat, straight and slightly toned and your shoulders relaxed and generally back and down. Do not tense up. Concentrate on your horse's well-being and watch his body language all the time. If he objects or seems worried, pass on and do something else, particularly if you have tried two or three times in one spot. You may be able to come back to it later.

Shiatsu movements

There are various movements in shiatsu and other techniques of bodywork which complement the major meridian work and which are detailed in the illustrations accompanying this section. Some of them make demands on the practitioner's body, particularly the back, so it is advisable to seek medical advice if you want to use them.

In themselves, they will help to improve your strength and suppleness as well as your horse's but if you have any existing weakness or injury you need to take the advice of a doctor or physiotherapist before performing those which would use the particular parts of your body which concern you. The (horse's) leg stretches and foot rotations, for instance, may be stressful to your back and knees, particularly with a horse who tends to lean on you till he is accustomed to this work. Do take care in this respect.

Here Vick is 'jiggling' Theo's foreleg to see the extent of relaxation of the muscles above the elbow. Squat down and hold the forearm near the knee with both hands and move it quickly forwards and back

Finishing off

To finish off any session, 'close down' the horse by repeating the stroking procedure. At the very end, I always put both hands round the dock, lift it gently and run the hair all the way through them, allowing it to drop against the horse's back legs. Horses I treat regularly then know that this is the end of the session.

You may find that horses unused to shiatsu walk away from you after, say, about twenty minutes, so do not carry on. As they come to understand, appreciate and welcome the therapy more they will stand for a full session of about an hour.

Forelegs

ABOVE: *To work the shoulder muscles, lift the foreleg and press inwards behind the shoulder blade. It is not easy to work muscles which are taut because the horse is using them for standing: when the leg is raised the muscles relax, making your work easier. Your own safety is paramount so horses who tend to lean on you should be corrected, as when picking out feet or shoeing*

OPPOSITE: *Janet is working meridians in Lucy's foreleg with fingertip pressure, her left hand being the control hand and her right hand the working hand. All the meridians can be worked in any area where there is a problem, to help get the energy moving*

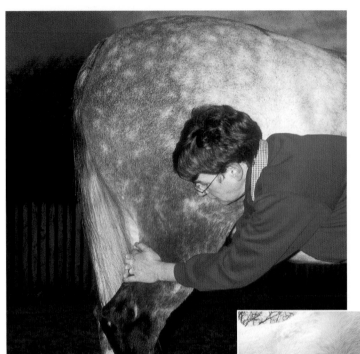

Hind legs

LEFT: *Jiggles are also performed on hind legs to check the state of relaxation of the thigh muscles. Stand facing the horse's tail and to the side of him and rock the hock and thigh from side to side. Persuade the horse to stand with his toe resting on the ground so that the muscles will not be taut and can move easily*

Feet

RIGHT: *There are several acupressure points around the coronets which can be worked along with the meridians for leg and foot problems. Just press gently but firmly with the fingertips (depending on whether or not the area is sore) to encourage energy movement. As always, keep one hand working and one as the control hand, as here*

LEFT: *When working meridians in the hind legs, stand or squat to the side and* in front *of the leg. You never know when a horse will kick out and this is usually backwards. You will know your own horse well enough to know whether or not he or she cow-kicks forwards and to the side as well*

RIGHT: *Rotations of the feet can help to correct stance and gaits (when done regularly, as with most things). Place the emphasis on the outward or inward pressure depending on what action or stance you wish to correct. For instance, for a horse who toes in you emphasise the outward rotation, and vice versa*

143

Working the tail (which is part of the spine, of course) has an effect on not only the horse's trunk but also even his neck. Hold the tail right up under the root next to the buttocks, resting the dock on the web of your hand between your thumb and first finger. Hold the dock in support with your other hand and gently work the dock round and round about three times each way. Most horses love tail work once they are used to it; it increases relaxation and trust

Chopping with the sides of alternate hands not only redistributes blocked energy (jitsu) and gets it moving but loosens up the muscles and stimulates the meridians in the area treated. Pressure from the forearms all along the back, loin and hindquarter muscles similarly stimulates energy flow and balance in this very hard worked part of the horse's body

STRETCHING

One of the many things I love watching horses do is have a good stretch after getting up. Some stretch like a cat whilst others are more restrained.

They stretch by leaning back with their front legs out, their backs down and their heads up, also by stretching first one hind leg then the other, stretching their head and neck up and out at the same time, and they also stretch by standing on all four hooves, arching the back and neck up and bringing the chin in towards the chest. Sometimes they will then have a shake.

This apparently natural stretching routine, not necessarily in that order, seems to cover the horse's whole body, all the joints and soft tissues which need attention after inactivity or pressure, such as when lying down. Stretching and rolling are nature's idea of self-help for horses, helping to maintain the tissues in good order and making the horse feel good. Therefore, it is essential, and basic good horse management, to make sure that they have enough room in their stables to do this, that they are not hampered by clothing which discourages them and that they have ample free time on an inviting surface (turf, sand or an arena surface which is not too hard) to perform these 'personal maintenance' routines at liberty in a field or other enclosed area.

We all appreciate a good stretch now and then, not only on getting up in the morning. Stretching is an established part of a human athlete's routine and is performed in a set routine of certain stretches for certain purposes. Every joint in the body and its associated soft-tissue structures (muscles, tendons, ligaments and connective tissues) really ought to be moved throughout its limits of movement daily to help maintain full flexibility over long periods. It is also best to do the main stretching routine after exercise, work or a massage when they are warmed up and pliable, although some careful stretches and movements help a horse to prepare for warm-up and work.

Why stretch?

Why is it necessary to stretch after work? Surely the tissues have just been exercised and used and don't need any further manipulation of any kind?

During work, muscles have been working and building up waste products as a result of 'burning' the fuel in them to provide energy. Although slow trotting and then walking after hard work helps in their elimination by keeping the circulation going long enough for really effective removal of toxins, this does not do much for any muscle 'kinks' or knots which may have developed. The natural reaction of hard-worked muscles is to not only remain slightly contracted in this way but also to contract or tense up more to protect any tiny injuries from movement which may cause pain. Massage and stretching both help to avoid this situation by encouraging the tissue to relax. Muscles which are always in some degree of shortening either unremitting tension or spasm also tire easily and, so, become even more easily injured.

When insidious tendon injuries occur, it can often be because the tendon tissue has been put under stress due to an associated slightly shortened muscle not having been able to stretch sufficiently. In peak work (for a horse's level of fitness), various parts of the horse's body are asked to stretch. The only tissue which can really accommodate this stretch is muscle tissue. If it does not stretch far enough, the tendon takes the strain of the extra pull, which may be just too much for it, and injury can occur.

Stretching – Legs

OPPOSITE: *Stretching is now a regular part of the routine of most top equine (and human) athletes. To stretch a foreleg forwards, separate your feet so that you have a good and safe base of support, pick up the leg as for picking out and support the leg behind knee and fetlock. Pull it forwards carefully and if the horse resists just hold the leg there, if you can. If he makes a fuss, put the leg down if you can, rather than dropping it, which leaves you in control of the situation. Try again, talking to the horse. You will sense how far is comfortable for the horse. Hold it at his comfort point for a couple of seconds and then bring it a little further forwards. Then put the leg down. Trained therapists hold the stretches for various periods of time and a therapist should be willing to teach you how to do this*

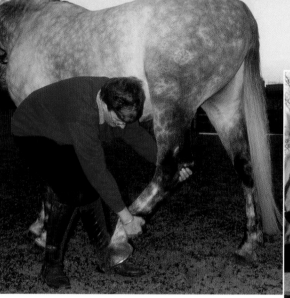

LEFT: *To stretch a hind leg, stand facing the tail, pick up the foot as for picking out, support the leg under the hock and fetlock and take your weight on to your back foot, bringing the leg with you. With any stretch in a horse unused to it, be happy with a little way at first. Ask the horse to hold the position for a couple of seconds, then try to bring it more forward just a touch, and put the leg down*

RIGHT: *Legs should also be stretched backwards, but most owners would want instruction from a trained therapist before trying this. Here, Janet is at a mid-way point with one of Lucy's forelegs. She has kept the forearm vertical (the horse's instinct is to angle it forwards, bending the knee) and the cannon and pastern horizontal, supporting under the joint for comfort and reassurance for Lucy. This will stretch the muscles and soft tissues down the front of Lucy's leg. The next stage would be to simultaneously lower the hoof almost to the ground and gently encourage the knee back with the left hand holding it underneath, and applying gentle pressure to Lucy's forearm with Janet's left upper arm. Put the hoof on the ground after a second or two and praise the horse*

Another way in which injuries can occur is when muscular imbalance develops. No horse is perfectly 'straight' and probably no rider rides equally evenly on both sides. Add to these two facts a saddle which was fine for the horse when it was initially fitted but which has not, of course, changed with the horse's muscle development, and it is easy to see how imbalances can occur with use over time. They can arise because exercise and gymnastic schooling, including active stretching such as lateral work and correct way of going, are limited or done incorrectly and the horse uses and develops the wrong muscles for the task requested.

Insufficient exercise for whatever reason is also a clear cause of injury because the rider may push the horse to perform feats for which he is simply unprepared. This can easily result in over-use due to a rider who is too enthusiastic and demanding and who does not recognise the subtle signs the horse may be giving that the work being asked is too much. The athletic horse must use his tissues and body correctly most days of the week if tissues are to be maintained in such a state as to not only perform but also resist injury.

Ligaments are of great importance in maintaining the body of the horse in good physical condition. They are the main structures which stabilise joints and allow them to flex and extend without overdoing it. If the horse does overdo it it is usually because we have expected him to do so. Ligaments themselves are only very slightly elastic but do respond to correct stretching exercises.

In the days when equine athletes were routinely fully body brushed and systematically wisped, problems of muscles remaining to a lesser or greater extent in spasm must presumably have been fewer than in those of today's horses who are not properly body brushed and never wisped. Now, however, it seems that only the best-run racing yards with traditional backgrounds habitually use strapping so there is a need for some method of relaxing and 'restoring' muscle tissue after work. This can be done by means of massage and stretching. In my experience, even in days gone by stretching was not done on horses (as opposed to wisping as a form of massage) and has only attained prominence in human athletic maintenance and therapy during the last twenty years. It has always been an essential part of classical ballet training, however.

This knowledge has been passed on to the horse world and, sensibly done, stretching is a great help in maintaining suppleness and mobility and, therefore, of helping to achieve physical comfort and optimal performance levels whether the horse concerned is a family, mainly weekend mount or a world-level athlete. As a therapeutic technique, it is a valuable tool for owner-riders to use to help prevent injury which can occur if muscles in even slight spasm or tension are worked beyond their present limit.

Most horses can benefit from stretches (and other therapies) and there are active and passive stretches. Active stretches are those in which the horse is expected to use his own muscles and perform the stretch himself, such as ridden exercises or those where he is expected to stretch his own neck by reaching up, down or to the side for a titbit. Passive stretches are those which the handler performs on or for the horse such as the neck stretches and leg stretches.

(The opposite of stretches is, of course, flexion. The controversial subject of flexion tests during veterinary examinations has made many owners doubtful about flexion exercises and it is certainly the best plan to discuss with a therapist suitable ones for an owner to apply. Particularly tricky are those flexing the shoulders and hips, which can also be risky for the unpractised back of an owner.)

In this book only basic stretching exercises are recommended and the author also does not advise untrained owners to try to take a stretch beyond its end of range without tuition from their therapist. Although the legs can move both backwards and forwards and also sideways out to the sides (abduction) and in underneath the body (adduction), these latter two movements can, again, be risky for an untrained handler, both from a performance viewpoint and judging how far to take them. A good and understanding therapist should be glad to help an owner with this matter.

Uses of stretching

- Specific stretches help to prepare tissues for work.
- Maintaining looseness and flexibility in muscles and other soft tissues after work, so helping to avoid stiffness, muscle 'shortening', reduced range of movement, spasm and cramp.
- Keeping joints flexible and capable of their full range of movement.
- Helping to keep tissues, particularly muscle tissue, correctly aligned and, through increased suppleness, evenly developed and balanced.
- Helping to keep muscles 'on the ball' and so increase the speed with which they can react to messages and adapt to work. This increases their shock-absorbing ability which is important all over the body but particularly in the forehand: the ribcage is suspended by soft tissue in a 'thoracic sling' as there is no joint between the shoulders and the ribcage, so healthy, toned-up muscles assist the strong functioning of this structure.
- Helping to promote elimination from the tissues of waste products, particularly after work, by 'loosening' up the muscles so that blood and lymph can flow easily and normally through the tissues.
- To assist in restoring comfort and normal state and function after stressful situations such as hard or taxing work, farriery or travelling. It is rarely realised how the latter two activities can stress the horse's body as he uses his muscles to counteract abnormal posture and muscle use.
- Enhancing the relationship between horse and handler and encouraging the horse to co-operate in his handling and management. Horses who are used to being 'handled' or physically manipulated in this way are normally much more amenable to other practices carried out in their care.
- Increasing flexibility, bodily comfort and, therefore, willingness to work.
- Helping to keep resting horses loosened up and flexible; like most things in nature, anything which is not used ceases to operate to full capacity – or at all in some circumstances. Use it or lose it! Judicious stretching can and should be used on horses on box-rest (depending on their specific injury). Horses out at grass for a rest benefit from stretches to help maintain physical mobility beyond the level the horse would demand of himself. Older, retired animals can have their comfort increased by our helping them to remain flexible by performing careful, appropriate stretches on them with a therapist's advice.
- In summary, stretching greatly helps to keep the body healthy and comfortable by keeping it supple and flexible, facilitating the circulation of blood and lymph to provide nutrients and oxygen and remove waste products and debris. A body in this condition is much less susceptible to injury.

NB: It is vital never to stretch cold tissues or in areas of acute, painful injury or spasm as this can result in over-strain, tearing of tissues and fresh injury. Areas which have experienced acute muscle damage should be professionally assessed as to their level of healing and a therapist's advice taken as to whether or not stretching would be beneficial, and what stretches to use. After full warm-up, cooling down after exercise and/or after a thorough massage, stretches may be performed.

Preventative stretching

Stretching to 'iron out' any small knots or muscle spasms which may exist after work helps prevent these becoming more significant and serious through more and more surrounding tissues becoming involved. A stitch in time saves nine, as it were. Stretching to maintain alignment and freedom enables the area to receive a full blood supply. Although only one part of the horse may be affected, this is often hard for the handler to spot so it is safest to stretch all areas and watch carefully for any signs of resistance in the horse which may indicate undue stiffness, pain and, therefore, a small injury or muscle spasm.

Performing stretches before other procedures than work such as travelling and farriery, which can both be quite stressful mentally and physically, puts the body in the best condition to cope with the demands to come. Stretching afterwards serves the same purpose as after work.

Remedial stretching

If a horse has had an injury, it is well worthwhile having him treated by a physiotherapist or equine sports masseur/se who may well give you some safe and simple stretches to perform yourself to keep up the good work. If not, ask, because there is much you can do to help the process. If your therapist declines to show you any techniques or give you any explanations of what to do and why, try another therapist.

If a horse has injured a particular part of his body, other parts will be taking the strain by moving in what is called a 'compensatory' way – using muscles not usually used to, say, walk normally, and bearing more weight on other parts to relieve the injured part. This can certainly cause injury to those tissues which can be prevented or lessened by good physical techniques such as massage and stretching. However, the stretches used depend on the horse's injury and what he is capable of standing at that time, so it is important to have professional advice in such circumstances.

Movement range

Muscles have maximum and minimum ranges of movement: the maximum range or end-of-range is the limit to which the leg or joint can be taken without stressing it and most horses will certainly let you know this by resisting or blocking the stretch when it starts to be felt. Once the limb relaxes, it usually can be taken fractionally further which will actually stretch the tissues a little, and this is all that should be aimed for. Over-stretching can certainly cause injury. If the horse objects or even looks uncomfortable, retreat a little and maybe just hold the limb in position before replacing it on the ground. Taking things slowly and gradually will accustom the horse to stretching as part of his routine.

The maximum shortening or contraction of which a muscle is capable is, obviously, the other end of the scale. Most muscles work most easily somewhere in between the two and it is natural for the horse not to wish to make too much effort in this regard. However, the less tissues are taken to either end of their range the less they become able to reach it. From the point of view of maintaining optimum suppleness and flexibility, therefore, stretching is needed; from the point of view of strength, contraction against resistance (weight) is needed as in the horse's own bodyweight, hill work, pole work, transitions and gymnastic dressage and jumping exercise whatever is the horse's main discipline.

The length of time a stretch is sustained depends, again, on the experience of the horse and your therapist's advice. The first part of a stretch can be held for up to ten seconds after which time, provided you have not hassled the horse or employed force, the horse will hopefully have relaxed the limb into the position and you should be able to take it *fractionally* further and hold it for ten to twenty seconds, although the horse may well not permit this in the early days. Holding the stretch sends messages to the body to adapt itself to this position and, as it were, allow the tissues to be gently stretched, so that it becomes easier and more effective in the future.

(Readers of this book may have noted that shiatsu stretches described previously are not sustained in this way, but they are undoubtedly effective particularly for loosening up a horse before exercise.)

Handler's posture

The average riding and driving horse will weigh around half a ton/tonne which is, of course, much heavier than the average human. Horses unused to stretching routines may lean on the handler and this can certainly cause injury if the handler accepts this. I find that teaching horses the word 'no' for all situations in which the horse is doing something I do not want is valuable for stretching, too. If a horse starts to lean on me I say a firm but quiet 'no' and if the weight becomes significant I do stop, albeit trying to put the leg down rather than dropping it, as a means of controlling the tissues and to some extent disciplining the horse. Some say that this teaches the horse that if he leans on you you will stop but I find that a second's reassurance before trying again in fact teaches the horse that he is not going to be hurt, that he may not lean on you and that you are not going to give up, but you may compromise.

Always do this work in a large loosebox as the horse is more likely to be quiet and well-behaved there than in a field or open space. Ideally there should be someone loosely holding the horse for gentle restraint. Make sure you have strong footwear and that the floor is non-slip. Keep your feet apart to give yourself a strong base of support and do not put yourself in a position where, should the horse move, you will fall or lose your balance, which is very dangerous around horses. Use your knees rather than your back to lift and support your back by leaning your nearest elbow on your thigh. Do not stiffen up against the horse but try to flow in a relaxed, toned way with his movement. It is safer to bend from your hip joints, not to round your back or crouch: keep your back straight and flat and your neck extended up from it and tuck your bottom in.

Preparation

Although stretching, massaging and generally working physically with horses is hard work and makes you strong and fit in itself, it is wise to increase your bodily strength and flexibility before taking it up as a human body completely unprepared is no match for the level of strength and activity involved in working with even a well behaved horse. You must realise that the horse only has to give a little spook, pull back, lean on you or argue and you can overstress your own body by trying to compensate for it, the back and shoulders being the most vulnerable areas but also the knees if they are not particularly strong. Horses often object somewhat when they are unused to being exercised/stretched in this way and if you are not very tactful and strong, this is when accidents can happen.

Before starting a session, relax yourself, centre your attention on the job in hand and do some slow, deep breathing exercises. Supple up your own body by rotating the shoulders back and forth slowly and as far as they will go without strain. Be calm and positive.

151

Exercises for suppling

The word 'supple' may be defined as 'pliant' and suppleness as 'freedom of movement'; the word 'stiff' may be defined as 'lack of flexibility' and 'stiffness' as 'unyielding'. The body, whether human or equine, will be quick to tell its owner what condition it is in! Stiffness is not exactly pain but it can verge on it. Stiffness is uncommon, in its extreme, in younger animals. Their tissues contain more fluid than those of older animals and will probably have experienced fewer injuries. Injured parts will subsequently feature at least some scar tissue which is fibrous, less flexible and more easily injured than the original and older animals, particularly those who have worked, can be expected to have old injuries, scar tissues and less flexible tissues in general.

Stretching – Tail

BELOW LEFT AND RIGHT: *Stretching the tail to the side is done by standing to the side of the hindquarters and gently stretching the tail down and sideways to both sides, normally using both hands. Hold for a few seconds and return it*

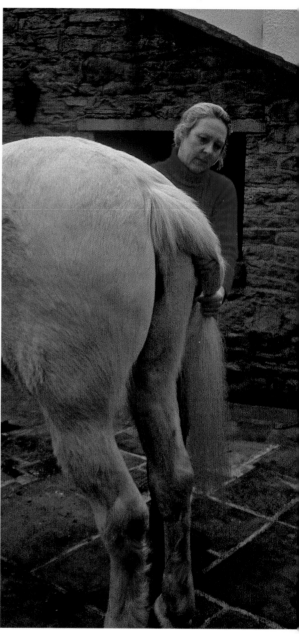

OPPOSITE: *Carefully stretching the tail is beneficial for the whole spine when correctly done. Of course, if your horse is known to kick you should not perform this movement. Stand behind him with your feet spaced to front and back as shown for stability and safety. Hold the* dock *(not just the tail hair) with one hand above the other and lean back on to your back foot, so using your weight on the tail rather than pulling it. The ideal situation is for the horse to drop his head and lean forward against the backward feel but Theo here is too interested in watching his owner. A friend with a food treat is helpful here. Hold the stretch for about five seconds, then* slowly *release your weight and put the tail down*

153

Suppling up the horse before work can include stretching all four legs forwards and back *but not to the ends of their ranges* and holding for five or six seconds, ten if the horse will permit. The neck can be stretched upwards (often overlooked) and downwards by asking the horse to reach for a carrot and also to the sides. It is important not to torment and tease the horse in this work; maintain these stretches for five seconds only and when he seems to have stretched as far as he reasonably can give him his reward. To do otherwise can result in resentment which you certainly do not want.

After the horse is warmed up you can dismount and do some end of range stretches, if you wish, as the passive ones will certainly help the horse to work freely and help to limit the chances of injury due to over-stretching during work.

Mounted exercises for suppling during work, which can be done instead, include circles from 20m down to 10m if the horse is capable of these, pole work and hill work. Poles on the ground are only moderately taxing so they can, with advantage, be raised at one or both ends either on wooden or plastic blocks or on the bottom retaining board of the manège.

Simple lateral work can be done even on unfit and green horses with a bit of practice. The horse should be obedient to the word 'over' and you can move the hindquarters and shoulders over both ways in the box. When mounted, according to the horse's level of schooling, excellent lateral exercises to both stretch and strengthen the abductor and adductor muscles are turn on the forehand, turn on the haunches, leg yielding, shoulder out and shoulder in. These *must* be performed correctly to be of benefit physically and to further the horse's schooling so a competent and sympathetic teacher is needed. It is particularly important not to over-flex the horse with the inside rein and to control the outside shoulder with the outside rein and outside leg on the girth, so that the horse does actually move laterally and does not just do a diagonal, straight line towards the track. Particularly when learning this work, the rider sometimes cannot feel the lateral nature of the work, which is why a good teacher is needed.

After work, end of range stretches should be performed to 'iron out' any kinks or minor spasms which may be forming. This will greatly reduce any feeling of stiffness some hours after work, or the next day. This practice is also helpful in maintaining muscle balance, posture and even function: you may have no idea if a horse is suffering from a minor ache or pain from working (as opposed to a noticeable pull, tear or other injury) and careful, considerate stretching of legs and neck, like an athlete or dancer, will help keep the horse comfortable and supple.

To the horse, any induced exercise is work. Whether he has been doing groundwork (with or without some persuasive training aid), competing, hunting, going for an active hack or schooling in a manège on the flat or over jumps, he will benefit from stretches afterwards.

Even horses who are not in work but on box rest or out in the field, including those pensioned off fully or partly, will benefit from being stretched appropriately. Older horses are often left to get on with retirement whereas this is often just the time when they need to be kept physically supple so that they may enjoy their lives. Standing in a cold environment, too, tenses up the muscles for long periods at a time and this is not suitable management for older or resting horses. Better facilities plus appropriate stretching about three times a week will improve the quality of their lives considerably.

When thinking about stretching exercises and movements for injured horses, do take advice because he may not be able to use his body to balance properly when you are stretching the non-injured area and stretching an acutely injured part is wrong. Such horses may well benefit more from massage, shiatsu, grooming, judicious wisping and so on to help keep their muscles in good condition, to stimulate their circulation and energy and to feel still part of things. Horses definitely know when they are 'out of it'.

TELLINGTON TOUCH

A remarkable system of riding, groundwork and touch therapy has been devised over many years of study by Canadian Linda Tellington-Jones. This entire system is unlike any of the 'natural horsemanship' systems and is one of the author's favourites. Practitioner training is available and there are qualified practitioners in several countries now, including the UK. As with most methods, working with a trained practitioner is always a good idea, at least in the early days and for 'top-ups' when needed.

TTeam Work

The system known as TTEAM (Telling Touch Equine Awareness Method) must by now have helped thousands of horses, ponies and owners (and other animals, too) all over the world to overcome behavioural, emotional and physical problems on the ground, under saddle and in many varying situations. As a classical riding teacher I have used TTeam principles in my teaching (although stressing that I am not a qualified practitioner) mainly for groundwork and have found it very helpful for getting horses' attention and actually improving their attention spans, making them think what they are doing and where they are putting their feet and listening to their owner/handler, often in an enquiring way. The owners always comment that their horses are calmer and more 'connected' with them after this work.

Linda states that her methods are based on the principles of classical riding and the Feldenkrais method which is a method of helping people to achieve 'postural awareness' and to become aware of exactly how they are moving. It also involves correcting incorrect or unbalanced movements and posture by means of gentle exercises incorporating non-habitual movements, i.e. movements which the person does not use often if at all. She applied these principles to horses and later, due to her interest in both 'cellular intelligence' and equine massage, she expanded her system further.

(Cellular intelligence may be said to be the ability of individual cells to react to stimuli and also to 'remember' how they have functioned and moved in the past: when an injury occurs and the body moves in a different way, the cells continue to function and move in this way after the injury has healed. The person or animal may not be aware of this and this can cause problems.)

Linda has found it possible to change a horse's behaviour and influence its personality without coercion or the constant repetition which many trainers use by using non-threatening and non-habitual movements of the horse's body plus special ground exercises which are detailed in her books, given in the Reading List.

Certain items of equipment are used with TTeam but these can be obtained from the address in the Appendix at the back of this book.

TTouches

Linda states that the Tellington TTouch 'influences the nervous system, instigates learning by activating the body's cells, integrates body and mind, and, as a result, encourages a state of health'. She also feels that the TTouch 'has a magical dynamic – as though it's a secret, wordless language between you and your horse'.

The TTouch method comprises a series of varied, circular touches of the fingers and hands which is intended to stimulate the cells to function and to produce an intimate communication and understanding between horse and handler or rider.

The TTouches are named after animals because animals inspire Linda and she connects each animal's personality or style of movement with a TTouch which she feels has similar qualities.

It is advised that, as with shiatsu and massage, the handler first strokes the horse all over to settle and relax him, get him used to being touched pleasantly all over and so that the handler can detect any areas of heat, tension, soreness and so on. The horse will usually react in some way, even very subtly, when such areas are touched or approached, so the handler should keep an eye on his body language all the time.

After this preliminary stroking, it is advised that a 'fingertip exploration' is done to seek out such areas. The fingers are held in a softly 'hooked' posture and, following a stroke to warn the horse, gentle pressure is applied with the fingertips (not the pads, so you need short nails) into the area and immediately off again, checking the horse's reaction all the time. The areas to concentrate on are the topline and muscular areas of the neck, in front of the shoulder, the shoulder muscles, the muscles of the forearm, the girth area, along the back and hindquarters and the muscles of the gaskin.

Pressure is described on a scale of one to nine, one being very light and nine being firm. This scale is used for further exploration of the body in lines or zones described on the head, neck and body.

Linda advises that the TTouches be used on horses with no problems just as a way of increasing intimacy and understanding between horse and owner, to encourage and increase relaxation, improve athletic ability and generally help the horse-human relationship and performance.

The basic TTouch is called *the Clouded Leopard*. It is said to increase a horse's self-confidence, reduce stress and help alleviate back and muscle pain, tension and over-sensitivity. Good also for horses who, for instance, are hard to catch or who won't stand still for mounting, it is normally performed on the horse's face and on the upper part of his neck, back and hindquarters, and also on the legs.

The hand is gently curved and the fingers close together. The pads of the fingers and thumb are used. Place your other hand a comfortable distance away from the hand you are using which helps with energy connection, stand with your feet a comfortable distance apart and be well balanced and relaxed yourself, with soft shoulders, arms and hands. Apply the touch, in the first instance, on a part of the body the horse does not object to having touched.

The technique is to use normally clockwise, small circles about the size of a 10p coin. Place your finger pads on the skin and, starting at six o'clock on an imaginary clock face, move the skin over the underlying tissues in a one and a quarter circle, finishing just before nine o'clock, so that you start and finish with an upward lift to the movement. Do not move your thumb but press it gently in one place to stabilise the finger movement. It is important to move the skin with the fingers and not slide the fingers over the skin.

If this TTouch is done quickly (say one per second) it has a stimulating effect on the horse but if you want to calm him do it as slowly as one TTouch per three seconds. I find this touch particularly useful for calming ridden horses and getting the head down in a relaxed mode. Just lean forward and do the touch on the top of the neck just behind the ears. I also say 'head down' which the horse should understand.

Try different pressures and speeds and note your horse's responses for future reference. This is also important in areas your horse may not like to have touched. Keep everything relaxed and flowing. You can do this TTouch to calm or stimulate a horse before or after work or ground exercises, the slightly heavier pressures and faster speeds being suitable for stimulation and vice versa.

When you have done one TTouch, slide your fingers to the next spot a couple of inches away, repeat, move on, and so on, carrying on for several minutes.

Several other touches and techniques are detailed in Linda's books as well as methods of teaching horses to stand still in cross-ties (not much used in Britain), to overcome dislike of being girthed up, to ease tiredness, tension, pain and shock, to help overcome head-shyness, biting, ease colic and stiffness in the spine, and other situations.

TTeam groundwork

The special groundwork exercises and movements are meant to improve behaviour and various physical problems such as nervousness, inability to perform certain movements and the like by improving a horse's perception of his world, his balance and co-ordination, his ability and willingness to learn and his overall outlook. Several of my clients to whom I have introduced TTeam have found a definite improvement in their horses' attitudes to life subsequently, as if, one said, the penny had finally dropped.

The chain, lead line/rope and wand

In America and Australia it is fairly common to lead horses with what I call a nose chain but which may also be called a chain shank or a stud (stallion) chain, for extra control and attention from the horse. I used to have a Thoroughbred mare whom I would never dream of leading in a public place (such as down the road to her field) without a nose chain because she certainly had insufficient respect for an ordinary headcollar and no matter how much you may trust a horse you just never know what they are going to do or what they are going to react to, often things of which we are not aware but which they sense due to their sight and hearing which are different from ours. I also find that you have more control with a nose chain than with an ordinary snaffle bridle.

As with many items of equipment, it is possible to abuse a horse with a nose chain. It must always be used sensitively and clearly in a 'feel-and-release' way, when horses previously unused to it will respond to it with increasing understanding. Horses must never be tied up with a nose chain.

An alternative to the chain is available, called the Zephyr Lead, which simply replaces the chain part of the lead with a soft rope. This is suitable for people who are anxious about using the chain, for young horses and very sensitive ones. I have had success with both items.

The chain or Zephyr Lead, lead line and wand, as they are called, are fundamental to TTeam groundwork and can be obtained from the address in the Appendix. Their use is shown in the illustrations. The total length of the lead line plus chain is about 8ft 6in or 2.5m.

If you have problems acquiring a proper Tellington chain lead or Zephyr, you can improvise well enough by using a heavyweight dog choke chain (what an awful expression!) fitted as shown plus an ordinary leadrope of at least 6ft or nearly 2 m in length and preferably longer. When using this arrangement, I prefer to use a lead rope of 12ft or almost 4 metres. This also makes it easier to perform the Tellington lungeing system if you are not quite as agile as you used to be. Because the chain fastens under the chin (both rings being passed through the chin ring of the headcollar) rather than running out of one side dee, you do not need to change it over when you wish to lead your horse from the other side.

(It is amazing how many people still regard the right side as the 'wrong' side from which to lead a horse. Horses should certainly learn to be led and handled from both sides equally, and to be mounted and dismounted from both sides, all for practical reasons. Horses also need to be taught everything from both sides – just because you can do something with a horse from one side does not mean that he will accept it from the other side.)

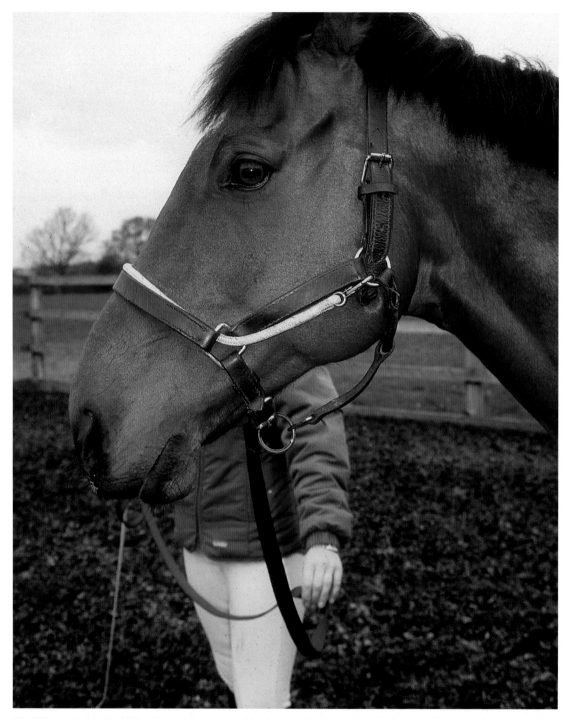

The TTeam Zephyr lead. The clip attaches to one side of the headcollar and the lead passes down the cheek, through the lower ring and around the noseband

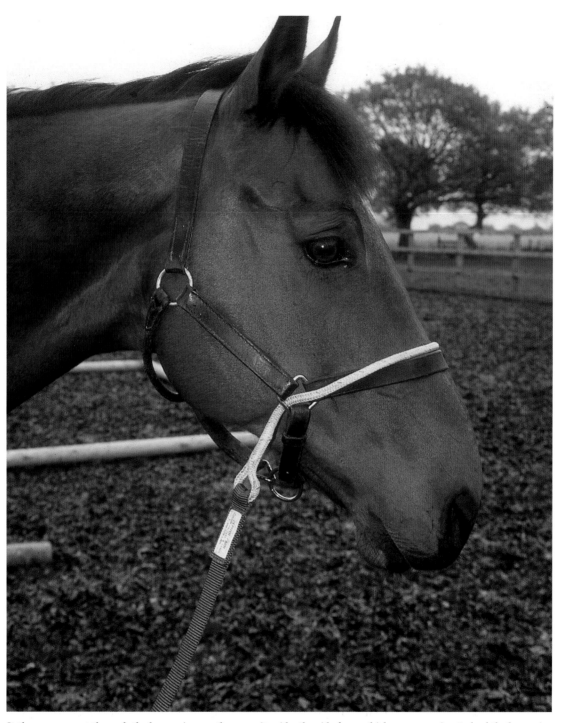

It then passes out through the lower ring on the opposite side, the side from which you are going to lead the horse, in this case the right side

The TTeam chain lead is the same design as the Zephyr but the soft part of the lead is replaced by a chain. For the benefit of UK readers, leading from a chain lead is common in the USA. An improvisation is shown here using a heavyweight dog chain. It passes through the jaw ring of the headcollar or, if a little short as here, over the strap, through the side ring, winds round the noseband, passes through the ring on the other side and back below the jaw. The leadrope is clipped to the rings of the chain as shown, not to the headcollar ring

One useful thing you cannot do with the improvised equipment is use it in the way Linda advises to *lower the horse's head*. I recommend to all my clients that they teach their horses the 'head down' request whether on the ground or in the saddle. It really does seem to have the effect of calming and relaxing the horse and helps him to feel more secure in his interaction with his owner.

To do this with the Tellington equipment, the chain is not fitted over the nose but is passed through one of the bottom side dees, up the side of the head through the ring at eye level and back down again through the other side of the lower dee, clipping to itself just below the dee. This (for some reason I have never been able to work out!) really does help to encourage the horse to lower his head and keep it down – so useful in many fraught situations.

The white wand is a particularly useful and effective guide to the horse. Presumably because of its colour, horses really take notice of it and it does seem to focus their attention and calm them. It is used to point out to the horse where he is required to go or what he needs to look at and to stroke the horse in specified ways to calm, instruct and guide him. I find it also very useful to hack out with as drivers seem to take more notice of it than an ordinary whip and give you more clearance. The term wand is used to avoid the possible connection of 'whip' with 'punishment' although, of course, the schooling whip should not be used in this way but as, again, a guide and extension of the rider's hand or leg.

When your horse is kitted out in his Tellington gear, the lead is normally held in your hand furthest from the horse so if you are on his left side the lead is in your left hand and vice versa. The wand is held in your free hand.

To ask the horse to walk forward you first stroke his back firmly two or three times with the wand then tap his croup the same number of times, at the same time giving his recognised vocal request to 'walk on', releasing any pressure on the chain or lead at the same time. I find this slightly elaborate method works wonders on horses reluctant to co-operate in hand and who just will not walk nicely with their handler.

To stop the horse, you tap his chest three times and give him whatever command he recognises to stop. (I use 'stand' and find it invaluable in any situation where I just want the horse to stand still. As soon as an experienced horse hears the S sound, it will usually stop and stand, waiting to know what to do next.) At the same time, give a very light, brief feel on the chain as a signal, releasing it immediately. *Never keep up a sustained feel on the chain and certainly do not pull on it or jab hard.* If the horse does not stop, just repeat the process until he does.

For difficult horses, you can fix the chain for leading from one side and the Zephyr Lead from the other so that you have a handler on both sides.

The different leading positions also have animal names and are used for different purposes. Because they are non-habitual (the Feldenkrais influence) they encourage the horse to think and absorb learning in a new way, to find his own balance without the weight of a rider, to realise that lightening his forehand makes movement easier and to listen to his handler and wait for instructions before moving – an invaluable lesson.

The ground exercises are all aimed at improving the horse's self-confidence, body awareness, concentration and communication with his handler. They involve taking the horse through shapes such as a maze and a zig zag made of poles. Poles can also be laid in a star shape and in a Pick-Up Sticks, random-looking formation, all aimed at helping the horse to concentrate and look and think about where he is putting his feet. The horse learns to lower his head, use his brain and flex his body and legs and to increase his own precision in movement.

The improvised chain in place

Walking over a wooden platform and a low see-saw are also interesting as is teaching the horse to walk over and between plastic sheets, which may eventually be over his head, police horse-style.

The basic leading position is *the Elegant Elephant*, good for everyday use but also for horses who are not easy to lead. The chain or Zephyr are in place and the end of the lead held in the hand furthest from the horse. Never wrap it round your hand but do make a loop of any extra length which can be quickly let out should you need to do this. Have the wand in this same hand held about half-way down its length. Stand slightly ahead of the horse, and slightly angled towards him, holding the part of the lead where the chain attaches with your free hand.

With the head of the wand, indicate the route you wish the horse to follow and give the normal signal to 'walk on'. Walk with the horse in this way until you want to stop. Then stay at your horse's head and say whatever command, long drawn out, you use to stop him. Hold the tone till the horse stops. You can slowly move the head of the wand up and down about twenty inches or fifty centimetres in front of his face. Also give his opposite shoulder a light tap with the head of the wand and give a light, quick feel on the chain.

Cyril follows where Tracey points with the wand and goes with his head well down, stretching his topline

Cyril easily negotiates the maze, following the wand

OPPOSITE: *Riding through the maze makes the horse really think about his posture and where he is putting his feet. Negotiating the corners is particularly good for both horse and rider, emphasising how much more effective it is to ride with the seat, legs and mind rather than trying to pull the horse round the corners with the inside rein*

Pauline tries the Elegant Elephant leading position with Rose

Cyril wonders what the star is all about, watching the wand …

… then walks on confidently

Another useful piece of TTeam equipment is this braided neck rope which is useful for helping to steady and stop horses

There are various other leading positions for different purposes, but if you only learn the Clouded Leopard TTouch and the Elegant Elephant leading position you will have added a useful and new dimension to your knowledge and ability to handle and educate your horse.

Two interesting and intriguing items of equipment are the body wrap and the body rope – intriguing because you cannot possibly see how they can work until you try them. They can be used for riding or for groundwork and both seem to work by bringing the horse into correct balance, physically but also mentally. I have found them very helpful.

The body wrap is made from work bandages in a stretchy figure-of-eight structure. Tie one bandage round the base of the horse's neck/shoulder area and fasten it with a knot, then attach one end of the second bandage to the knot and pass it carefully round the horse's hindquarters under the tail, like a fillet string, and tie the other end to the first bandage about fifteen inches or forty centimetres from the first knot, so that there is a length or 'bridge' of bandage passing over the back just behind the withers. The whole thing should fit snugly but not tightly and, if formed correctly, it will not slip. It seems to hug the horse and comfort nervous horses, slowing down those who go forward rather faster than you might want when being lunged, during groundwork or under saddle. It also reassures horses who do not like going through narrow spaces or standing for veterinary attention or farriery.

Rose and Pauline have a successful attempt at TTeam lungeing

The body rope is a lightweight rope, again fitted in a figure-of-eight way, and is used for horses who may seem stubborn or lazy, encouraging free-er, forward movement and co-operation. It lightly flops against the backs of his gaskins as he moves and really perks up overly-placid horses.

With both these items, it is important to ensure that they are not frightened by feeling them behind their hind legs. Horses these days are generally used to leg straps and fillet strings in this position so should not give trouble, but it is best to be sure by carefully fitting them and watching the horse's reaction all the time.

TTeam riding

The basic principles of classical riding and TTeam work well together – it is 'riding with awareness', having fun and using a balanced seat.

The riding can include riding with a neck ring and no bridle. A neck ring is stiff rope joined to make it adjustable which is used round the bottom of the horse's neck. The TTeam white 'wand' (a white schooling-length whip) helps with guidance. The horse obviously needs some preliminary schooling under expert supervision for this kind of riding. It is claimed that it develops trust between horse and rider, improves the horse's balance by giving him freedom and also helps the horse's natural gaits, his attitude and relaxation.

Another useful item is a balance rein – a braided circular rope again used round the base of the neck to help slow down horses who do not respond well to the bit (it really does help!). It is also good for horses who go on the forehand or have trouble lowering their heads and necks under saddle which is the basis of all good riding.

Riding bareback is another old and familiar technique. Linda explains that it improves the rider's balance and co-ordination and, without doubt, his or her feel. Once the rider is reasonably confident it definitely helps to improve the seat and posture, in the author's opinion as a teacher; the crucial point is to not stiffen up and raise the legs although this also applies to riding without stirrups.

Some of the other TTeam equipment used for the groundwork can be used under saddle, such as the body wrap and the body rope (see above) and the groundwork exercises can be performed under saddle although I prefer to accustom the horse to them on the ground first. If the horse learns to really think about what he is doing on the ground, it is much easier for him to do this later when he has a rider on his back to think about. A useful transitionary stage for inexperienced horses is to add a passive rider whilst still being led from the ground by a handler. As with conventional methods, the rider gradually takes over. When I use this method, I act as the ground handler and ask the owner to take over the riding.

CONCLUSION

I really hope that readers have found at least some therapies and management techniques which will be of interest to them in this book, and maybe some of which they have never previously heard.

As any kind of 'special' treatment becomes more and more specialised, many owners feel that they are helpless as regards their horse's health treatment but this need not be so. It is best to learn as much as you can and to be ready to quiz and push the specialists you use to give you answers you can understand. Your horse is yours and, in the UK, you are both morally and legally responsible for his welfare even if he is kept in someone else's care. Also, one way or the other, you are paying the bills! You do not have to wash your hands of technical matters but can take part in understanding what is happening to him, how you can help him and in actual hands-on, practical techniques which can help matters along whether in sickness, injury or health maintenance.

APPENDIX 1

READING LIST

Books go out of print and are reprinted or revised all the time. It is always well worthwhile asking a good bookseller to search for out of print books. As for in-print books, any decent bookseller can trace a book for you. Libraries, of course, are excellent sources of books both in and out of print and often sell off some of their stock.

Equine Injury, Therapy and Rehabilitation (Blackwell Science), by Mary Bromiley, and any other books by this author

The Art of Lungeing and *The Art of Long Reining* (J.A. Allen), by Sylvia Stanier, LVO

Enlightened Equitation (David & Charles), by Heather Moffett

The Classical Rider (J.A. Allen) by Sylvia Loch, and any other books by this author

100 Ways to Improve Your Riding and *How Your Horse Works* (David & Charles) by Susan McBane

Conformation for the Purpose (Swan Hill) by Susan McBane

Complementary Therapies for Horse and Rider (David & Charles) by McBane and Davis

Essential Oils for Horses (J.A. Allen) by Caroline Faith

Shiatsu Therapy for Horses (J.A. Allen) by Pamela Hannay

The Injury-Free Horse (David & Charles) by Amanda Sutton and any other books by this author

Improve Your Horse's Well-Being (Kenilworth Press) by Linda Tellington-Jones and any other books by this author

The Healthy Horse (Swan Hill) by Janet Eley

100 Ways To Improve Your Horse's Health (David & Charles) by Susan McBane

APPENDIX 2

Useful Addresses

Association of Chartered Physiotherapists in
Animal Therapy
Morland House
Salters Lane
Winchester
Hampshire
SO22 5JP

British Equine Veterinary Association
Wakefield House
46 High Street
Sawston
Cambridgeshire
CB2 4BG

Society of Master Saddlers
Kettles Farm
Mickfield
Stowmarket
Suffolk

Farriers Registration Council
Sefton House
Adam Court
Newark Road
Peterborough
Cambs
PE1 5PP

Equine Behaviour Forum
Grove Cottage
Brinkley
Newmarket
Suffolk
CB8 0SF
Tel: 01638 507502

The British Equestrian Trade Association
Stockeld Park
Wetherby
N. Yorks
LS22 4AW

The Equine Shiatsu Association
St Peter's Stud
Church Lane
Upper Beeding
West Sussex
BN44 3HP

The Equine Aromatherapy Association
PO Box 19
Hay-on-Wye
Hereford
HR3 5AE

The Classical Riding Club
Eden Hall
Kelso
Roxburghshire
Scotland
TD5 7QD

Equine Sports Massage Association
17 Gloucester Rd
Stratton
Cirencester
GL7 2LB

Tellington Touch Equine Awareness Method
Tilley Farm
Timsbury Rd
Farnborough
Bath
Somerset
BA2 0AB

INDEX